Milena Origgi

the WAY of the VOICE

A secret is hiding on everyone's lips

Dedicated to

Graziella

and

Antonio

Copyright © 2018 Milena Origgi

© 2018 INBORN VOICE
e-mail: thewayofthevoice@inbornvoice.com
www.inbornvoice.com

Translation by: Luigi Cuco

All rights reserved. No part of this book, text, photographs or illustrations may be reproduced or transmitted in any form or by any means by print, photoprint, microfilm, microfiche, photocopier, internet or in any way known or as yet unknown, or stored in a retrieval system, without written permission obtained beforehand from Inborn Voice.

The publishers and author can accept no responsibility for any consequences arising from the information, advice or instructions given in this publication.

A secret is hiding on everyone's lips

INDEX

1 How to become a guru?   1
2 Everything is vibration   33
3 A deafening silence   55
4 The laws of the world   73
5 The human voice   97
6 One, none, or one hundred thousand?   129
7 The twelve energies   155
8 The way of the voice   181

Acknowledgements   203
Contacts   205

1
How to become a guru?

Turn yourselves into a light

In the world in which we live, everything comes from a seed. A seed is a pure and concentrated essence: it possesses, from the moment it begins to exist, everything it takes to grow and evolve into something wonderfully more complex.

Each seed is born with an outer shell, leathery and resistant, whose task is to protect the inner soul from the outer elements. The inner soul is in fact something delicate, pure, that requires love, nourishment, and protection to be able to develop.

Each seed has the same chance of growing as any other, but everyone's chances change a lot depending on the conditions it finds in the place where it falls: more or less fertile soil, poor, adequate or excessive irrigation, light and heat measured at the right point and, why not, even a good dose of luck.

Nature teaches us that the strongest and most luxuriant plants are those that have managed to grow in difficult conditions, facing adversity with great pride and determination, not those that have immediately found the ideal conditions for their development.

If any of you were to try to calculate mathematically all the variables that contribute to create the probability that a seed thrown at random, sprouts and manages to bear fruit, you would be immediately discouraged. Not so much from the difficulty of calculation, but from the result: in fact, the probability of success in favor of the small seed is so low that every result can only be considered amazing.

In reality, the small seed is unaware of how unlikely it is to survive and mature. He simply knows that Mother Nature has enclosed everything that is necessary to succeed in himself. Somehow, we can say that the seed "has faith" in nature. In fact, the little seed has no idea what the fate might be, for him simply "there are no accidents" and is therefore ready to use all its energy to germinate exactly where he fell.

For my part, ever since I came out wailing, I have fallen madly in love with my voice. Probably that wailing was also my first "song". From that moment on, I let this love grow, like a small seed, day after day, trusting that in the end, everything would go for the better.

My first memories are all about singing. I have always wanted to sing, to share my voice with others. In my life I have never wanted to do anything else.

Today many young people who contact me are convinced that they have the same drive, yet this is not always the case. They are often influenced by the mass of information they constantly receive from the media. They perceive in themselves a strong resonance with the very idea of singing, but in reality, it is something deeper which they are not yet able to recognize. In the seventies the world was smaller than it is today. There weren't so many external influences, such as television shows, music videos, smartphones or the Internet, that could influence my will. In my family there were no artists, indeed the very idea of an artist's life was seen as full of hardships, always begging for money.

This was one of the first differences I noticed between myself and other children. Since I was a child, I have always had very clear ideas about my place in the world, despite all the hardships from family, school, and friends. The other children, depending on their moods or the hero of the moment, changed they mind continuously. One day the fireman, one day the dancer, the mechanic or a mother.

Almost all the children around me, instead of letting their seed blossom, to discover what kind of talent they had inside, chose to hide it from the world, almost with shame. More or less everyone preferred to adopt the idea of their parents who wished them to become a lawyer, an engineer, a doctor or a dentist.

Many children actually managed to become what they imposed on themselves, but this led them to feel empty, unhappy, full of fears or anger.

As I grew up I never changed my mind about my future, although I became fully aware of what my talent really was at my coming of age.

At the moment I simply felt the need to sing. I sang every day: I invented melodies, words, and rhythms. Of course, like every little seed, I also had my good dose of "luck", if we want to call it that way. I had a family and grandparents who never forced me to be silent. Today more and more parents, educators and reference figures are trying to silence children, perhaps because they themselves had been silenced as children. They might not want to hear something that they have kept hidden for a long time and enclosed deep within themselves as if a child's voice had the power to resonate with something childish that remained locked inside each of them.

I hope that anyone who has managed to read these few lines will become aware that silencing children is the worst thing we can do. It is even worse than giving them a good spank. We have all learned very well at our own expense how harmful a word can be, especially if it is said by someone dear to us.

Try to imagine what a defenseless child might feel when he tries to communicate his essence to the world, using sounds and words that he has found it hard to learn, especially when he is told by his parents, his entire universe, to be "silent". They are actually preventing him from discovering himself and the world.

Luckily, I could sing and I did so in total freedom. The whole neighborhood knew me as the "singing girl" and still today, when I meet some of them in the streets of my city, they remember when they stopped under the windows of my house to listen to me singing.

For me it was as if the music was in the air that surrounded me at all times: I was simply a sort of radio, endowed with the extraordinary ability to grasp it and repeat it.

During my childhood, I never had any great problems. Today I can assess the past, but at the time I simply went to school, sang and lived carefreely. Nothing more.

I am now aware that modern society, particularly the one in which children grow up, is still dominated by what we might call masculine "energy". Thankfully things are slowly changing: it could not be otherwise.

The very survival of our species, the entire evolution of the society that sprang from it, was a direct consequence of the energies employed by the physically dominant being, that is, the male of our species. Everything was imagined, conceived and built by a man.

Male energy is something that resounds strongly with logic, with the transformation of existing matter, with the imposition of one's dominion through force or division. They are all very good qualities, but very different from the kind of energy that emanates from the feminine.

A woman's energy is a vibration that resounds strongly with love and patience, that tries to create something from scratch and that wants to look at things with deep insight.

Modern women continue to grow and develop surrounded by this masculine "footprint" and much of what they do, suffer the consequences, dispersing part of their energy. For example, when women struggled to achieve their independence and equality, they simply adopted the present system, conceived with male energies, and expanded it to their sex. They did not ask for a moment if this was suitable for them if it resonated with the feminine vision of things.

In this I am certainly a pioneer: I was the first woman to create a method of vocal teaching with a maternal imprint, radically different from the classical one, conceived and developed by men in an era in which only males could sing and act in theatres.

Only as I grew up did I realize that everything around me possessed something that clashed with my understanding of the world. Society pretended to measure me and everyone else by the same yardstick, imposing an equal judgment for everyone, which took no account of anything but the final result of an obstacle course, designed for a specific type of person.

We have all been treated equally. Every one of us is born with an essence, a way of being, incompatible with the rigid demands of slotting envisaged by society.

This type of society leads, not by accident, the weak to give in to social conformity and surrender their uniqueness in exchange for the recognition and love of others. They simply adapt to the system, trying to compete to the best of their ability.

Children are under this pressure too, and the strategy that almost everyone adopts, sooner or later, is to begin to lie. To lie to oneself and to all others, building from scratch a new personality capable of replacing and keeping well hidden one's own essence. Each child was a seed that instead of choosing to sprout and venture outside its own protective shell, chose to develop another outer shell, even harder and more leathery than the previous one, to hide from the world.

This conformism generates a chain effect in all the others. Over time even the strongest tend to give up their essence as they realize the homogeneity already present in all other people, who gradually become the majority. Somehow they begin to fear being "different", to be afraid of the weight of others' judgment and the consequent "suffering" involved.

In practice, this perverse mechanism leads the strongest, the last to adapt to the rules imposed by society, to become the weakest. In fact, they have developed their essence for longer than others, so to keep it hidden they are forced to build a larger armor, whose maintenance involves a greater waste of energy. The more the essence is developed, the stronger it will be felt from inside the armor.

As nature teaches us, little by little, even the smallest roots of a tree are able to break up even the hardest rock in which they grow. Gradually, with time, their essence will be more and more intrusive and will do everything to show itself again to the world.

Today I also find it funny to note that the people who consider themselves the most "unique and special", are the same ones who care most about being the same as everyone else, a sign that something must not have really gone in the right direction.

An interesting fact is that at the same time as the development of the initial personality, the first nicknames begin to appear. Nicknames are a clear indication of the creation of a new type of individual who will then take the reins of a person's life. If you have a nickname that you have had since your childhood, to which you are even sentimentally attached, there is a good chance that the nickname itself will suggest to you what you can affectionately indicate as your "capital crime", the one that will distract you from your realization.

In my case, my essence has never stopped growing and vibrating loud and clear, thanks to the feminine energy that distinguishes me. I have never chosen to conform to what is imposed by society and I have managed to develop my essence intact, making it grow every day with me.

This choice, which for me was quite natural, led me to be radically different from the people around. My way of being has never been opposed by my loved ones. For the others, I was simply a maverick, a person with very peculiar tastes and able to bear the judgment of others.

From the fact of dressing up with very showy garments and colors to the choice of singing in church only as a pleasure and not as a duty, from not drinking any alcoholic beverage to not wanting children, these are just some of the decisions that characterize me. Only as I grew did I realize that many of these life choices were truly particular and different from those adopted by the majority, but today I am what I am thanks to them.

While growing, also the desire to sing has grown and I have always seized every opportunity to do so, with or without an audience. From the church choir at the age of 8 to the Punk groups of adolescence, from village fairs to major international competitions: I have never given up. In the course of my life, I have also participated in various musical projects and I have had the good luck to meet many fantastic musicians and composers.

Anyone can recognize that I have never missed the musical note of determination throughout this period. When a person has the musical note of determination and is committed to making it resound loudly, he can always achieve whatever goal he wants. The important thing is to remember that all this must not depend, even to a small extent, on someone else's commitment or decision!

When I started singing in public venues, I was still a minor. The bands I sang with were mostly made up of men who were at least five years older than me. It was then that I began to notice that somehow my presence, my voice, was able to move in people something dormant, asleep: like the sound of an alarm clock.

My voice seemed able to transmit messages capable of reaching a hidden part of people. My voice was already destined to resonate with their more intimate emotions, something that they themselves had long since stopped listening to. It almost seemed that my voice was able to create resonances and trigger new vibrations in a different plane from that of everyday life.

Those were the first symptoms that made me understand that my vocation was linked to the voice, but it was something deeper than simply singing.

Very often the people present at my performances came personally to greet me full of emotions, feelings and memories, which they could no longer contain. They felt the need to communicate them to me immediately, before they faded away.

Among other things, these fortuitous encounters almost always brought oddities, coincidences or other interesting anecdotes. In fact, sooner or later people all began to tell me about their deepest existential problems, without paying too much attention to the atmosphere of the place, to my young age or to the situation. They did it, and that is all.

I took this very seriously and even if I did

not understand what happened during these encounters, almost everyone returned to listen to me singing a second time just to thank me for somehow having "helped" them. At the time, I was a little girl and was still not aware of what or how I helped them: I was simply happy to do it.

I kept growing, singing and studying music. The English lyrics and my natural curiosity pushed me to deepen my knowledge of foreign languages even outside of compulsory schooling. Continuing in this direction, I enrolled in university to the faculty of foreign languages and literatures. At the time, enrolling in the music faculty did not resonate with me at all. It seemed more useful and interesting to me to continue the studies made so far. In fact, I was already aware that the best way to learn a foreign language was to go directly to the country where it vibrates in the voices of all those who speak it. During my university period, I had the ardor and insistence to ask my family to send me to attend a College in Cambridge (England), for a couple of years, where I then studied English with great ease.

At the time it was a rare occurrence, which only a few lucky people could afford. Obviously, during my stay abroad there were many coincidences, which only now can I recognize as part of a much more complex and intricate plan: the work of fate.

In particular, I have made friends with wonderful people from all over the world with whom I am still in contact. The College's multi-ethnic environment, attended by students from Turkey, Arabia, Argentina and Japan, served me well to understand how different vocal forms of communication can be. At that time I developed an interest in pictographic languages (i.e. those that do not use words to express the thought, but symbols).

So I began to study Japanese as well, a language that I still find fascinating in its oral form, but above all in its written form. Until then I had not fully realized the idea that all words, even those composed by the letters of the alphabet, were actually just symbols.

When I reached adulthood, the so-called "age of wisdom," something unconsciously changed inside me. That's the age when the head, pretends to be the "boss", to decide and control everything. For me, as with most teenagers, things had become too complicated. Like everyone else I tried to give a logical explanation to everything and consequently, to want to predict and control everything around me.

I could clearly sense a very strong push in a very precise direction. My head was convinced that my vocation was to sing and clearly this destiny, for the moment, no longer depended on my willpower alone.

At that time, I didn't have the experience and vision I have today, in fact, I was convinced that my gift was just to sing. I always wanted to sing, I wanted to record more music, I wanted to participate in more competitions. The more I did, the less it was enough for me. Singing led me to shoot like a spinning top in a world that never changes, even if full of interesting people. Singing had become a routine that didn't go to my heart anymore. I wasn't interested in fame and success, I just wanted to sing!

It was as if I had fallen into deep sleep, yet I was quite sure that I was neither Snow White nor Sleeping Beauty. I continued to feel within myself a need, an intimate and profound need to which I was not able to give a name or an explanation. In time this need was transformed into a suffering that pulsed, rhythmically within me, every moment of the day and night.

It's a feeling you can only understand if you've already experienced it firsthand. It is similar to the fear of having forgotten something, when you are not yet aware of having done so, to the feeling you have when you want to wake up from a dream and you fail, or to the feeling of having an inner void that never fills, whatever you do or eat.

In short, it wasn't a good feeling at all.

This type of sensation always leads to great inner crises and great research of practical solutions. At that time of my life, in an attempt to find what I felt had been lost, I approached and studied many Eastern disciplines, thanks to the advice and the friendships developed around the world.

Why Eastern cultures disciplines? Maybe because they are the most frequent, the ones that still maintain a veil of romanticism, a kind of mysterious taste, but more than anything because I was practically certain that whatever I was looking for, it was out there.

After reading, experimenting and learning a lot in so many different areas, my research stopped. Not because I had found what I was looking for. Quite the opposite. The East and its disciplines had not been able to give any conclusion to my research. On the contrary, the opposite had happened. They had opened up so many other questions that I could not answer. It was as if I knew that everything I read, learned and knew was incomplete or distorted. As if the very essence of information, the key to understanding everything, had been dispersed over the centuries. A piece was always missing. It was as if the blanket I tried to cover myself with was too small. Pulling it on one side, I discovered myself on the other.

In an attempt to fill that feeling of inner emptiness I have done what many other people do: I have continued to throw into myself new studies, new ideas, new theories. I tried to give peace, to silence that inner feeling, filling my life.

I did not realize that my physical body was not able to handle all the information and knowledge that I pretended to slip into it. Probably my demands were too many. I don't think Albert Einstein would have been able to do that either!

I thank my father yet again for having shaken me up and diverted me away from what had become endless research that I had taken upon myself driven by the desire to fill my inner emptiness. He forced me to take a job at his factory, giving me time to pause and stop searching, by doing something practical.

Respecting the simplicity of life, I was able to understand that what I had perceived as an emptiness, was actually a huge sounding board. It was only amplifying something I held within myself, to let me perceive it loud and clear. What I had forgotten was simply to listen to my essence.

It was at that time that I had my first illumination. I understood that the problem was not that it was impossible to find answers to the questions I had asked myself. In fact, anyone I had asked about some of my questions, be it a luminary or a simple friend, would have been able to give me his very personal answer. And each answer, as always, would have brought with it a sequence of new and endless questions.

I finally understood that answers are not a rare and precious commodity. For every question, you can find endless answers. When one seeks an answer to a question that arises from within, one cannot find it outside. People's answers or the knowledge transmitted by books inevitably become a subjective version of what "perhaps", originally, was the objective answer I was looking for.

Taking a break, I began to listen inside myself and I finally understood. It is not important to find the answers: it is the answers that find us. The important thing is to ask yourself the right question!

At that point, I was sure there was no way out of the labyrinth of notions and contradictions in which I went hunting during my research.

If I wanted to emerge victoriously, I would have to take a new path, one that was different from all I could learn from the outside world.

I found the main road, the one capable of bringing my vibration into this world, within myself. All the efforts I made to try to find a solution and fill the inner void were as useless as they were harmful. They kept me busy and therefore prevented me from listening to what was already inside me and wanted to blossom outwards. Rather than seeking answers to questions from outside, you just had to listen to the only question arising from inside. There is no universal answer, just a personal question.

Inside of me shone a light capable of taking me, one step at a time, out of the darkness that surrounded me. Like a child starting to walk, the first steps were the most uncertain. Over time I understood that my internal light had the ability to make transparent the veil that prevents, in most cases, to see beyond the appearance of exteriority. At last, I was beginning to know my essence from within.

At that precise moment, I became aware

that I had hidden a small "guru" inside me. In Sanskrit, *GU* expresses the concept of *darkness*, while *RU* expresses that of *light*. Combining the two terms you get the ability to disperse the darkness.

Philosophically speaking, darkness cannot be aware of its form or of its very existence until it encounters its opposite, that is, the light. Inside each of us shines a small light and it is our duty to find it and bring it to light the darkness that surrounds us. Once brought outside, it will light up your way, to make you take the right choices, to show you what makes it brighter and what instead tends to turn it off.

And because when things move in the right direction, it's very difficult to stop them, from this first illumination, I've come a long way. My little *guru* was able to ignite my awareness, my conscience and my desire to be the mother of a new teaching, born, raised and developed solely with female energy.

Clearly a little *guru*, like a small lantern, also needs those who take her around the world, to show everyone what can be done with a little faith in themselves. When you're on the right track, you'll also meet the right people, and all the elements seem to magically fit together in a giant planetary puzzle.

In my case, the title of Guru (गुरू) was given to me affectionately by my students. Far from me is the idea of being a saint or a person with superhuman powers, but since there are no accidents, I have adopted it with pleasure.

In fact, the *guru*, apart from the mystical meaning known to the majority, is actually a very particular type of teacher: the one who understands and knows perfectly a unique and specific art. In my case, the art of voice.

One of the questions that are asked most often by my clients after I find their voice with my teachings, perhaps after years of previous unsuccessful attempts with the more traditional ones, is where I studied and learned to be a voice "Guru". It doesn't matter whether they're businessmen, ordinary people or famous singers, their curiosity is always the same.

The answer that comes out of my lips is not what is expected.

I have studied and I still study today, subjects typically related to the use of the voice, but also many other parallel themes, from the scientific medical field to the more holistic Eastern disciplines. My knowledge is not limited to the minimum necessary because I set myself the task of covering the world of voice at three hundred and sixty degrees, nothing excluded.

I also read many books and magazines. Yet I can say with certainty that so far, none of what I have read or studied is part of my art.

Of course, every notion I add can serve me or my clients, who are happy to find within me more professional figures, but all I have learned is not the essence of what I do. I can't even say that I learned from the experience of mentors: I started singing as a self-taught person and I never took lessons to learn how to speak, sing or act with anyone.

Actually, when I explain the origin of my art, I always start by stressing that it is precisely the word "learn" that is unsuitable. Learning is about being taught something through the use of the intellect, and those who have had the privilege to work with me know perfectly well that my whole teaching method is something very far from this idea. In fact, it is not technically possible to return to using our voice in the correct way using the intellect: another way is required.

Sometimes I compare my work with that of a luthier. For those who do not know, the luthier, a professional figure in extinction, is the craftsman who makes by hand the lutes (i.e. the stringed musical instruments, such as violins). Among the most famous violin makers in the world, we can boast Antonio Stradivari. You will all have heard his violins mentioned, if for no other reason than the enormous economic value they have. They are universally recognized as miracles: the sound they produce is something that technology still fails to replicate. This is a perfect case to understand how a science, specifically acoustics, is not able to replicate the mastery of a craftsman.

In fact, a true craftsman is able to stand out from those who learn only from books or teachers, because he was born with a natural gift that he developed with a good dose of patience and dedication. Stradivari personally chose every single component of his violins, the processing technique, the materials to be used and even the times to follow. Unfortunately, his recipe, his trade secrets died with him. Modern science can only observe that the secret is not identifiable in any specific part of its violins, but in their entirety. Stradivarius had a unique gift. He was able to listen to the essence of each piece of wood so that it could resonate perfectly.

My work is practically the same. In fact, I am a vocal coach who always chooses with whom to work and I apply all my art with care and dedication to transform each of my students into a perfectly tuned musical instrument, able to make their voice resonate in this world.

I have had the good luck, if we want to call it that way, of being born with a gift, a spontaneous and natural talent. My only merit has been to let it flourish without constrictions or preconceptions. Many other ancient or modern disciplines, including the scientific ones, were born the same way. For example, today you can study computer science, you can learn biology and even learn music from books.

All these disciplines, at the very beginning, had not been codified but were "created" from scratch, or better, from the passion and commitment of a few. Even the English language that allows you to read this book was born from the work and passion of a few and today is spoken by well over 1.5 billion people!

Having been able to preserve and develop my natural talent allows me to draw on some form of "superior" knowledge, in which I find answers and solutions to the vocal problems of the different client I meet. This ability is not something I have control over. I cannot get in command: on the contrary, I would say that it always happens and only when I do not request it. In some way, when I need it, I always find the answer, the exercise, the right question within me. Most of the time, this kind of inspiration happens when it really serves my clients when their will is strong enough to break down some invisible barriers.

As you can imagine, in my work I am mainly concerned with the voice of my client. I help them to rediscover a voice to love, to re-educate some forgotten mechanism, to make emotions flow through words, to find the courage to make their voice heard and much more. Some time ago I chose to name my working method, which is totally different from the traditional ones, *Inborn Voice*®.

The choice of the English language is linked to my desire to spread my knowledge as much as possible, although originally, I would never have thought of taking it in person to the United States. The choice of the term *Voice* is obvious, as I'm mainly in charge of it. The term *Inborn*, a word that very few Anglo-Americans already know and that I prefer not to explain too much to avoid influencing your opinion, you have to go in search of a deeper meaning that you will have clearer only after reading the whole book. Inborn means that everyone's voice has been "sown" within us by nature itself, just because we were born, it is not something that we acquire later. Even the symbol I chose for my first website, www.findyourvoice.guru in the early nineties, was a star anise seed: there are no accidents!

Reading this book you will better understand the origin of this philosophical choice, for the moment it is important to understand that *Inborn Voice* is a direct consequence of the interactions with my clients. Every time I meet a new client, since each person is unique, whether they want to learn to sing, speak or simply start a journey on the *way of the voice* with my guide, my method evolves and becomes, in some way, more complete. As I always explain, it is a method in continuous evolution and I am trying, step by step, to "codify" it in order to transmit it in the best possible way to others, without it being distorted or destroyed in its essence, as happened to many other disciplines, both technical and spiritual.

This book is a first attempt to put on paper something that goes beyond my very own way of teaching people how to use voice, but that is an integral part of it. I will venture to explain something complex, which is difficult to tell in words and probably part of what you will read in this book will remind you of something you have already read or heard differently. It is not uncommon for the same vibration to create resonances in several people and in different fields.

I am perfectly aware that the pure knowledge that lies within me cannot be transmitted to others by means of a book, but I would still like to show everyone the *way of the voice*, the only way to make blossom the essence of every human being who wants to become an active part to change himself and the world.

My essence is to help people connect with their own, opening up to the world to bring their miracle to fruition.

2
EVERYTHING IS VIBRATION

Nothing is lost, nothing is created

In the following pages, I will present some fundamental ideas to begin to glimpse, a little at a time, the existence of the *way of the voice*. It is not necessary to understand them all, indeed if you struggle to understand the meaning of something, it is a good sign! It is more important to have an overview of concepts than to have an exact definition of them. It is not my job to talk about such complex things, I hope you will forgive any inaccuracy.

The original form of everything that exists is pure energy. What we can perceive with our senses is energy. Today, thanks to technological progress, we can also add that all we can measure, thanks to some scientific instrument, is always and only energy. Almost everyone agrees on this point. From philosophy to religion, from physics to chemistry, no one has any doubts about this hypothesis anymore.

In recent decades modern physics has finally come to prove that matter, as we conceived it until a few decades ago, has never existed. Quantum physicists have been able to observe, measure and then intuit that all that exists is some form of energy. This revolution has given life to the new branch of quantum physics, which I am very passionate about.

Future generations will also appreciate how much this change will inevitably affect their daily lives, a bit like when science has managed to show that the Earth is not flat, or that it is our planet that orbits around the Sun (and not vice versa!).

Now we just have to understand what energy actually really is.

Every word we use every day is nothing more than a symbol, a container suitable for expressing part of an idea. A word must always be considered for what it wants to communicate, not for how it is proposed. In practice, there is no difference between an Egyptian hieroglyph, a Japanese logogram or the various symbols that surround us, such as the number 8 or the $ symbol: all serve only to express an idea.

Energy is a word that you have surely heard and used many times in your life, but perhaps you have never stopped to investigate its meaning. The idea connected to the word *energy* is the presence of something you can't see, something invisible, but something we are able to perceive its existence from the tangible effects it produces in our world.

Specifically, energy is defined as an active force, a force capable of altering the existing state of things.

A perfect example of energy is electricity: it is invisible, yet we can appreciate the lighting of a light bulb or the trill of a mobile phone. Another example is the muscular energy: our body moves as if pushed by magic. There are no wires or other tangible systems that explain, for example, our turning a page of this book.

As I have already said, the original form of all that exists is pure energy. In our earthly existence, we are not able to fully perceive or understand what "pure" energy actually is, we can only make assumptions. Even the most established quantum physicists do not fully understand its essence. This ambiguity is at the origin of the fact that the word *energy* is often used inappropriately or with fanciful conceptions, far removed from its natural meaning. Try to free your mind from the preconceptions you may have accumulated in your previous experiences to be able to fully understand the essence of this word.

It is not my intention to go into quantum physics or give too technical explanations: the only point that is important to understand now, is that all the forms of energy that have been observed by science with a good level of detail, also thanks to recent technological advances and the latest theories developed, have a property in common: all of them vibrate.

Let's understand what it means to vibrate.

The concept of vibration is something you can easily guess for yourself, just try to open your mind. The idea that sustains the word *vibration* is of something in continuous and unstoppable movement. The characteristic movement of a vibration depends on many factors, but in its essence is described as "coming and going". The washing machine during the spinning phase, the stereo case during the reproduction of a piece of music, the silent ringtone of the mobile phone, are all examples of vibrations that we can perceive through some of our senses, such as sight, touch or hearing. In reality, the idea of vibration expands well beyond mere sensory perceptions.

A form of vibration that more or less everyone has experienced in person at least once, is that of a rope stretched between two fixed points.

The clothesline for laying the laundry, an elastic band stretched between the fingers, the string of a guitar or a piano: these are all examples of a "thread" stretched between two fixed points. This type of vibration is called linear because it expands and exists only along the line created by the wire. From a mathematical point of view, the world of a tensioned string is composed of a *single* dimension, yet its vibration is capable of expressing itself in a further dimension, in a different plane, that is, in a two dimensional world. In practice, this means that vibration has the power to influence even something that goes beyond its very existence, for example, the air that surrounds it.

To conceive a vibration born in a *two* dimensional world, it is necessary to imagine, for example, the perfectly smooth surface of a pond or a lake. Throwing a stone into the water triggers a vibration. At the moment of impact, the stone creates a ripple around it to open a gap towards the bottom. The stone created only the first ripple. All the following ones, which expand concentrically along the surface, are just a consequence of it. Also, in this case, the vibration born in a two-dimensional world is expressed in a world with an extra dimension, that is three dimensions.

Clearly, things get very complicated as the number of dimensions increases. You will probably already have difficulty in understanding what I have tried to explain so far. Do not be discouraged, the important thing is to understand that we live in a world composed of at least three dimensions and that the result of the vibrations we create, whatever they may be, will also be expressed in a further dimension, not perceptible to us.

For the moment, just take the idea of "coming and going", typical of a vibration, and make it your own. Even the most gifted scientists have difficulty explaining in words what they perceive about the vibrations of the matter because when they observe the most elementary particles at their disposal, they notice something that does not correspond to anything that can be explained through rationality. For example, they notice that the particles disappear and then reappear, that they do not continue to move as expected in a straight line and above all that the very fact of observing them, affects their behavior. One day, perhaps, science will be able to explain these phenomena, for now, it limits itself to measuring and recording what are clearly the effects of some type of energy.

Throughout the book, I will try to explain many concepts using the idea of a guitar string. This same idea is the one used by modern physicists when they talk about the "string theory", a new theory that aims to put quantum mechanics in agreement with the general relativity of phenomena that we can understand. Don't be surprised if this thing is difficult to understand, it is, in fact, something that goes slightly beyond the capabilities of our brain: in fact, to grasp it fully, you have to use another "way".

The man has long intuited this nature of energy, even if science has only recently been able to demonstrate it. Plato described this vibration as the Music of Spheres (or Nature).

Every ancient culture has defined it in some

way. I like to define the pure energy as the *Voice of Silence*.

To cite just a few historical examples, in the Bible this concept is expressed with "In the beginning was the Word. The Word was with God and the Word was God. [...] All things were made by him and without him was not any thing made that was made".

This phrase, that sounds arcane, was written in a language that is now dead and then translated several times from one language to another until it reaches modern English. What can be read today, therefore, seems little comprehensible to anyone other than a theologian. Without going into religious details, this passage only explains the idea that everything that exists started from something that we can conceptualize as a *Word*. Now we need to understand again the idea, the concept that encloses the symbol of the word *Word*. The common use of this word has changed several times over the centuries, so things get complicated. Probably the first meaning you will find in your mind will lead you to an idea not corresponding to the meaning we are looking for. The meaning we are looking for is simply "to utter", to speak, or produce a sound.

Another passage in the Bible more effectively underlines the same idea, namely that in Genesis it is said: "God said: 'Let there be light!' ". In this passage, it is clear that it was the arrival of the vibration produced by a word in a world of absolute silence that created the light.

The basic idea that the ancient texts try to express in both cases, in a language and an example comprehensible to the majority of people of the time, is simply that of vibration.

First, there is silence, calm, and then there is a sound, a vibration. Philosophically, between the lines, they are simply explaining that all that has been created and exists, is a vibration, an active energy.

I mentioned the Bible because I was raised with Christian instruction, but whatever sacred text you read because of your curiosity or religion (the Torah, the Koran, the Nada Brahma or whatever), it tells the story of creation in the same way. The arrival of some form of vibration in a state of stillness has created everything.

Creation is described, more or less in the same way, also by atheist science, when it explains the concept of the Big Bang. In fact, a great explosion is no doubt a great source of vibration!

Although everything is energy in motion, in our human condition we can only perceive and study some aspects of it. It would be awesome to have at one's disposal some more sensory organs to be able to listen to the music of the universe, in its complex harmony, which continues to expand, create, evolve and perfect everything.

Maybe this sixth sense already exist.

In fact, many of our sayings make explicit reference to vibrations that we have somehow perceived. For example, when a particularly nasty or violent event occurs, we often find ourselves saying something like "I feel shaken". This very widespread way of saying was born to explain with a metaphor what people perceive pervading their whole body: a shock, or a strong vibration that resonates within us and that it is impossible not to notice.

At other times we find ourselves explaining the same idea with phrases like "I feel agitated" or "I have butterflies in my stomach". These are all expressions that try to communicate to others what is within us and that probably is simply a vibration. We also have ways of saying "I'm itching" or "I feel a tingling sensation". Again, all expressions that describe some sort of vibration.

In reality, these vibrations can also be perceived through the other senses, such as sight or hearing. How many times have you found yourself with your ears ringing, saying "someone is thinking about me". Once again, a vibration was perceived.

There are also other phrases that try to make us understand how some of our actions were the result of the external influence of a vibration, for example, "I acted with an impulse", "I had a shot of anger" or "I made a jump of joy". All these ideas show that in reality, we are continually subjected to some form of vibration of which we know very little.

It doesn't matter if it comes from inside, from the movement of the planets or from some arcane magic: we live them and almost always act under their influence, with no apparent possibility of escaping.

Well, now that you have begun to understand what energy is and how it is vibration, one last step is missing to have a clear idea of the whole.

It will be easy to guess that for the vibration to occur, it is also necessary that there be some kind of substance capable of responding to its solicitations. I'm not interested in defining which and how many types of "matter" can exist. The important thing is to understand that everything that exists is composed of some kind of original substance that in its evolutionary progress has given life to all the materials we know pervade the universe.

Understanding what this primordial substance is (i.e. the "purest" substance that surrounds us), goes far beyond all our possibilities of physical, mental and spiritual conception. Those who have studied some scientific subjects, such as chemistry or physics, will know perfectly well that the most complex substances are nothing more than the union of several atoms of simple substances. As you probably already know, water is a mixture of two hydrogen atoms and one oxygen atom. In turn, each atom is composed of more elementary particles. For example, oxygen is composed of eight protons, eight neutrons, and eight electrons.

Quantum physics is discovering, hypothesizing and studying even smaller particles that in turn contribute to compose protons, neutrons, and electrons. These substances have names that you have probably never heard of, such as *quarks*, *bosons*, *mesons* and so on. Don't be frightened by so many high-sounding terms. The important thing to remember that the more you go down in the small, the closer you get to the original matter, which pervades everything.

I do not intend to go any further with this speech, but it is also worth considering that science recognizes and measures the energy consumption that involves the creation of more complex substances, as well as how much energy is released by their destruction.

For example, a growing tree consumes the energy of the sun to make photosynthesis and become stronger and more robust. Then when its wood burns, the energy that had been stored is released in the form of heat.

Despite ourselves, science has rediscovered that it is also possible to break the most intimate bonds of molecules, those within a single atom. Although they are infinitely smaller, they contain unimaginable amounts of energy. You all know what a terrible power it is capable of triggering the explosion of an atomic bomb.

If you have followed me up to this point you will be quite clear that everything that exists and surrounds us is always matter in vibration.

Now it is enough to make another small effort to understand a deeper philosophical concept, often overlooked, but fundamental: the matter that exists, however immeasurable, has certainly a finite amount.

To better understand this, I will give you some examples using well known substances present on our planet. If we consider water, as we have seen, composed of two hydrogen atoms and one oxygen atom, we can find truly enormous quantities on our planet. We find it in the seas, in the lakes, in the subsoil and in the atmosphere. Even our body is more than half made up of simple water!

Although water is almost everywhere, it is still present in a finite quantity. Some have also had fun calculating that our planet carries around 332.5 million cubic miles of water. As you can see, it is such a huge amount that we cannot even compare it to anything we know.

If instead of water we consider gold, we all know that it is something rare and therefore precious. If we were to use all the gold extracted from the mines so far, we would only be able to fill 4 Olympic pools. This is a quantity that becomes easier to imagine!

Whatever the type of matter we take into consideration, whether it is a known chemical or something more subtle and intangible, we can certainly say that we have a more or less small amount of it at our disposal.

The last effort I ask you to make, to conclude

this chapter, is again to free your mind from the preconceptions that crowd it. We really need to understand that vibration is everything, literally everything that exists. In other words, there is nothing that is not some kind of vibrating matter.

Now I will give you some examples to give you the opportunity to expand this concept and make you appreciate the beauty of the creation that surrounds us.

Take a fish, for example. What is the difference between a fish swimming freely and happily in the sea and one on display at a supermarket counter? If you think about it for a moment, the first thing that catches your eye is that the first fish is alive, the second is dead. This is also evident to those who have never seen a live fish.

As I have made clear, vibration is everything, so we can safely deduce that life itself is some kind of matter in vibration. It is something that the human being can neither measure nor understand, yet he is able to appreciate and perceive its existence. As we saw at the beginning of the chapter, every phenomenon capable of producing tangible effects is, by definition, the result of some energy. In this case, we are talking about vital energy.

I find it wonderful to know that the closest form of "pure" energy to us is life itself: something so delicate and rare that it is even irreplaceable.

If you have understood this, it will be easy to expand the concept to other things we know for certain to "exist", even if only in our inner world. A feeling, an emotion, an idea, a pain: they are all capable of altering the state of things, so they are also a vibration.

Everything is vibration!

Do you begin to understand?

The force of gravity is a vibration, so much so that scientists define it as composed of gravitational waves. Even the idea you are making of this very complicated chapter is also a vibration, created artfully within you by my words. You have surely already heard about brainwaves!

In reality, the concept of vibration is much more complex than that of a simple "wave".

Our earthly existence will never be able

to understand the complexity of the subtlest vibrations. For example, it is already difficult for us to understand the fact that at this moment, by touching the pages of paper that make up the book, we are touching vibrating matter. Our perception is of something static because for our daily life it is not important to perceive and recognize these vibrations, but only those that really can be immediately useful to us.

In fact, we all manage to imagine and understand how every sound we perceive through our ears is a vibration that is transmitted through the air, just as light is a wave that is propagated through the void.

Probably the most educated of you will also know that every musical note corresponds to a particular frequency, or that each color corresponds a specific wavelength.

These concepts have been taught at school for almost a century and you will have heard them even though, in practice, no one has ever seen or heard a color or a sound as a pure and simple vibration.

Many other phenomena that surround us

are the result of a vibration or its resonance.

Resonance, as we will see later, is the ability of a vibration to trigger others. To resonate is nothing other than to respond to a vibration with another vibration, a bit like our voice does when it echoes in wide spaces.

If we expand the concept of vibration further, towards other characteristics of the world around us, it will be easy to accept that success is vibration, wealth is vibration, happiness is vibration. As I have already said, everything you can name is vibration.

Of course, everything is vibration, but not all the matter that vibrates is the same. There are countless types of them, more or less complex. For example, the vibration that generates wealth is clearly of a different type from the one that will generate success. We do not know these details, but every matter is present and available to us in limited quantities. The rarer the vibration, the rarer and more valuable is the matter.

It is essential to understand that not everything can be made available to everyone.

It is impossible for everyone to be happy

at the same time, just as it is impossible for everyone to be angry. It is impossible for everyone to be rich, just as it is impossible for everyone to be poor. The impossibility is given in the first place by the scarcity of matter that can generate certain vibrations. If we were to divide the gold on the planet equally between all human beings, no one would be rich. On the contrary, many would probably not even give value to the fact of owning some gold.

In order for a person to call himself rich in gold, he must possess much more gold than the average of the others! It takes a lot of patience and skill to be able to accumulate enough of it, collecting it from those who do not know what to do with it or how to manage it in the best possible way.

In the same way, for a person to be able to trigger the vibration "happiness" for himself or for someone else, he must first have accumulated a sufficient quantity of matter suitable to manage that type of vibration.

The impossibility is also given by the phenomena of resonance that inevitably come to be created when a new vibration is affirmed among the others. This will generate different effects, even opposite and contrary to what was hoped for. For example, if we consider happiness as a vibration, what would sadness be? Sadness is not simply the absence of the vibration of "happiness". Happiness and sadness are the result of different resonances in different "matters".

As you may have guessed, the world of vibrations is truly complex, but this does not mean that there are no universal forces and laws to which they too must submit.

Some of these are known to us and I will now try to introduce them to you.

3
A DEAFENING SILENCE

Compare your voice to endlessness silence

Let's begin this chapter by asking ourselves some questions. Have you ever wondered why you look like your parents and close relatives? Have you ever wondered why this similarity is not so only from the point of view of physical appearance but pushes you to have their habits, manias, fears, ideas, and way of reacting in front of life?

These are all interesting questions that, sooner or later, everyone comes to ask themselves at least once. Depending on your level of spiritual awareness or your level of scientific preparation, you can find different answers to these questions. As I have already made clear, answers are not a rare and valuable commodity. You can find as many as you want: genetics, social interactions, psychology and the list can go on indefinitely.

It takes little awareness to notice these coincidences, these resonances, in everyday life. It takes a little more to understand that even those who claim to have grown radically different from their parents, for example, because they could not stand their way of doing or being, in fact, is the consequence of a perfect resonance produced by the energy present in them.

To better understand this point we can consider an ancient way of saying that we use quite often: "opposites attract". This sentence underlines this very point. What appears to be a diametrically opposite difference is actually the other side of the same vibration, or rather a vibration opposite and contrary to what was somehow considered unbearable in your parents.

The questions never end, you should know.

Have you ever wondered why some people fail to succeed in the work field and/or with social relationships despite the excellent level of education they manage to achieve and all the commitment they seek to put into their lives?

Have you ever wondered why other people are able to achieve great success both economically and socially and moreover without any apparent effort, despite having almost completely neglected all forms of higher education?

Don't let your mind wander to look for examples that can confirm some of your ideas about this. I am referring to stereotyped visions that consider how easier it is to succeed when you are a "father's son". Stop and consider only yourself. You can be sure that you will never have the chance to know anyone better than yourself, even if at the present time it is very likely that you do not know yourself so well.

Have you ever wondered why, in spite of all

the energy and commitment you inject into your life, in an attempt to achieve some kind of result, from your very inviting and palatable point of view, you still fail to achieve it?

Have you noticed how everything you try to do, in the end, you almost always trigger the same pattern of events that then inevitably leads to different results than expected and probably not wanted?

Many of you will call this kind of experience "failure" or "insuccess". The word *failure* expresses the opposite idea of the word *success*.

Do you know what the idea of *success* is? It simply expresses the fact that something happens after a previous action. So *failure*, by definition, is when nothing happens as a result of an action. Then if the result is different from what is expected, it cannot be considered a failure, but it is technically always and only a *success*, even if it does not correspond to the desired one.

If you have been asking these questions for a long time or are starting to consider them only now, this book may lead you to guess their answer.

Of course, knowing the answer will be of no use. In fact, understanding why something happens is not necessary, nor is it sufficient to prevent it from happening again. If we gave a guitar all the awareness and intelligence needed to understand how a violin makes such a majestic sound, it would never be able to "transform" itself into a violin or produce that kind of sound. In order for the guitar to play in a similar way to the violin, as always in life, it will require the intervention of an external energy, for example, the intervention of a very witty luthier.

My answer to all these questions, and to many others, is simple: they are all phenomena of resonance.

Every beat of our heart is a miracle. Every breath we take is a mystery. Every single cell of our body, every star of the universe, breathes and has a heart that beats following a rhythm that is cadenced and unstoppable.

Yet we are not normally aware of our breathing or the beating of our heart. Everything happens almost unnoticed.

If we try to observe the infinitely small, for

example an atom, or the enormously large, for example our solar system, we are not able to appreciate the presence of a breath or a beating heart, since everything happens at speeds too fast or too slow for our understanding. This does not detract from the fact that everything around us pulsates and resounds.

As we have seen, everything is energy, everything is vibration. In such a complex system of organization, nothing can happen without this having an impact, even minimal and imperceptible, on everything else.

When we were conceived, we were only pure essence. The outside world had not yet shaped us. Our vital energy, our essence, was vigilant and free to express itself. We had not yet begun to create anything, surely none one of the many personalities we keep alive within ourselves today. Realizing how everything is the result of a resonance phenomenon, of vibrations created in response to others, is not easy. I will try to help you by telling you a little story.

Imagine introducing something delicate and precious, such as a small music box, into a large shed full of wooden fruit boxes. The small music box still knows nothing about itself, all is unknown. How could: it has not yet had the opportunity to do so. But it hears the other fruit boxes talking all around itself.

Every fruit box tells proudly how useful it is in the world, how beautiful it is to bring fruit to the market, how perfumed can be the fruit in the season or every other detail that makes itself feel useful and important. And they do this very loudly and continuously. Probably fruit crates don't like silence and as soon as they feel it around them, they instinctively fill it with useless chatter.

How do you think the small music box can be heard? Immersed in all that hustle and bustle, it won't even find the right opportunity to play and resonate its music. The music box probably thinks that, even if it ever tried to play some music, no one would listen to it.

Gradually it realized that it was different from everything else around and in itself the vibration of fear began to come forward. The fear of not being accepted, or worse, of being mocked by all the other boxes of fruit, especially those to which it cares most.

As time goes on, it thinks that this diversity only leads to sufferance. At a certain point, the music box will no longer want to endure the enormous suffering it feels and will direct all its energies into creating any trick that will bring itself back to a state of peace.

It is precisely at that moment that the small and delicate musical instrument, conceived perfect in every part, begins to no longer consider itself as such.

It begins to think that perhaps it was born as a music box by mistake. Perhaps it too should have been born as a sturdy box, perhaps for a very precious type of fruit, of those that there are very few to carry.

The small music box could rebel against not only its nature but even that of those around. With a sufficiently strong dose of suffering, the small music box might want to turn into something better than a box made of raw wood: for example a jewel box made of precious wood briar, full of colored and sparkling inlays. And if its vital energy is sufficient, it may indeed succeed. It would always be a wooden box, but what a wood! And it would not carry stinking fruit, but the best of the best: diamonds!

The soul, the original essence of the music box no longer has the opportunity to express itself. Even itself has forgotten to be a music box and all its vital energies are now used, not to bring music into the world, but to support and nourish the wooden shell that has been created all around. Indeed in its intimacy, the music box thinks that if it were hidden into a drawer or a safe, it would be even better.

More or less this is how the small music box participates in the silence. It simply tuned in and resonated with its surroundings. It doesn't remember being a music box: it is convinced to be a closed box, which can no longer be opened because the key has been lost who knows when and who knows where.

My gift is to have a bit of a master-key of these situations.

Yet there are no accidents, everything is the consequence of something else. If a music box was born between fruit boxes, it can not be an error. On the contrary, it was there that its music was most needed!

This little story tells what is likely to happen to us all. We resemble those around us not only for reasons related to chemical-physical factors but also because of the others vibrations that surround us. In fact, our essence, pure and strong at the moment of birth, if not supported by the right energy, tends to give way to the personalities that we develop naturally because of the phenomena of resonance with the sociocultural environment we live in.

I will try to explain this concept further, to give everyone the opportunity to understand the complexity of this phenomenon.

Music is something truly magical and is able to "resonate" within our body in ways that may seem mysterious, but that can become simple and fun to experience in person.

You have certainly felt sad in your life for some reason. For example, a sentimental delusion or a work disappointment. Generally, to avoid listening to the sound of the voice of silence that surrounds us, in those moments we listen to music.

Well, what kind of music did you listen to in moments of sadness? Perhaps something cheerful and carefree? I do not think so. You've heard music that resonated with your inner feelings, that is, something sad and poignant, or something that stimulated the spirit of revenge or payback.

And when you were really so happy, do you remember that music was always at hand? Certainly, the musical repertoire of moments of happiness is very different from that of sadness. A sad piece would seem too slow and boring in moments of happiness.

Another example is when you listen to music to give yourself a charge, to achieve some sporting or athletic goal. I doubt that in those moments you want to listen to the same music as when you are sad or when you are happy.

The music you want to listen to is the one that resonates most, the one that "tunes" best, with some vibrations already present at that moment within us.

This phenomenon has a dual reality, it allows us to know somehow empirically part of our inner vibrations and it also allows us to change them. In fact, there are several studies that highlight this aspect.

When you force yourself to listen to a type of music that isn't in tune with yourself, since you don't have control over that external vibration, our reaction is to "tune in" to the music. For example, if you are forced to listen to sad music long enough, you will soon become melancholy.

The power of this type of mechanism is such that many military organizations have adopted music to create real "torture" to induce prisoners to reveal their secrets.

Now that it's more clear what a resonance is and how it works at the vibration level, you'll also get a better understanding of the answers to the questions we asked ourselves at the beginning of the chapter.

Vibrations, in some way, behave as if they were a substance which nourishes us. We absorb them because of the resonance phenomena and they become part of us. Some of these vibrations are really easy to "move away" from, others are more persistent and it takes a lot of strength and determination to do so.

Without entering into too philosophical and profound aspects, it will be clear to you why you speak with a certain accent, with a particular cadence or with some typical lack of pronunciation, without you being aware of it at all or giving it any importance. Each parent, each reference figure, transfers part of his or her own vibrations to his or her children because of the resonance phenomenon.

Some are more obvious, others less.

The vocality of each of us has been trained through practical experiences and most of the time when you do not get the desired results in familiar, sentimental and professional relationships it is because your communication includes some inappropriate features that trigger a resonance inside the people around you.

My professional experience tells me that by simply intervening on a person's voice it is possible to help him change many of these "unsuitable" resonances that he has always carried within himself. Many of my greatest successes are related to people who wanted to simply remove their accent, their cadence or some pronunciation defect to appear more suitable and prepared for a promotion or a new job.

The important fact to note is that it was not me who chose to correct or improve their vocal skills. It was they who "felt" this need. They paid attention to some form of inner discomfort, a deep and negative resonance. And they have done a lot of work to achieve the results. I just helped them realign with their *Inborn Voice*.

Today it is increasingly rare to meet people who are willing to invest energy and sacrifice towards a higher goal. Being determined is not something difficult to do. Just be simply honest with yourself and keep a decision long enough so that its vibration can settle down.

Yet today it seems that everyone wants to get everything, quickly and even immediately! This kind of mentality, or rather vibration, has spread like wildfire over the years and has resonated in every aspect of our lives. Everything must necessarily be simple and within everyone's reach.

This vibration has its origins in our childhood. Trying to dig into our memory, trying to make an effort to remember the past, it will be easy to identify moments in which we all believed that we could do incredible things, without suffering fatigue, without sweating and without encountering any obstacles. Some will remember with a smile that they have lifted or moved enormous weights, that they have won a race with their fastest friends, that they have scored the victory goal with their favorite team, that they have communicated with a toy or with some pet. The luckiest will remember that they've done even more wonderful things, such as flying or having all the powers of a superhero.

Each of us has these memories more or less buried by years: I'm talking about dreams. We all dreamt of this kind of thing with our eyes wide open, when we were playing as children or when we grew up, during sleep.

During adolescence, human beings undergo

various changes, which lead them to activate a whole series of functions that were previously 'dormant'. Among these, there is also the part of the brain that is dedicated to rationality that should make us more aware of the objective reality in which we live. Reality is quite different from dreams. Without effort, commitment, dedication and the ability to direct our energies in the direction of our own talent, not much can be achieved.

Don't worry about the word *talent*, because each of us has at least one! And knowing how to look for it, it's not even difficult to find it.

That is why I describe people like being trapped in deep sleep, from which they seem not to really wanting to wake up, even when their own lives are put at risk.

Anyone who has ever participated in a marathon, knows how to paint a portrait, knows how to keep the charts of accounts of a company, knows perfectly how many years of preparation, sacrifices and pain, have passed under the bridges before reaching that level of expertise. Even people who excel in some field, have had to learn how to do it. A talent can lead to excellence, but it still needs to be nurtured. Among other things, it is not certain that developing one's talent leads to becoming rich and famous, but it certainly leads to the evolution or the creation of something that brings with it satisfaction and happiness.

When we face the world and its vibrant reality, a minimum of common sense is enough to understand that it takes almost always much more time and dedication than expected to obtain, when we succeed, the desired result.

The difference between someone who succeeds in achieving a result and one who does not is not only to be found in perseverance but in vibrations and resonances.

In our daily life, we give different names to these phenomena, for example, "chance" or "luck". While perseverance is important, it usually overstated and it is only a part of what is required.

In fact, if it is true that the people who achieve a result have fought to obtain it, it is also true that is not enough to fight to obtain a result. Very often those who have obtained a remarkable result have tried many other roads before finding the one that has given them the greatest satisfaction.

The typical reaction of people who are faced with the crudeness of reality is the same as we do while asleep during the night and someone turns on the light. We simply turn the face the other way to cover our eyes and to get back to sleep.

Over time, people age and stop trying to improve things, prefer to sleep and live in peace. And when you live without willing to improve things, everything that happens is really the result of accident. You behave, without awareness, like a sailboat driven by the will of the wind and sea currents.

4
THE LAWS OF THE WORLD

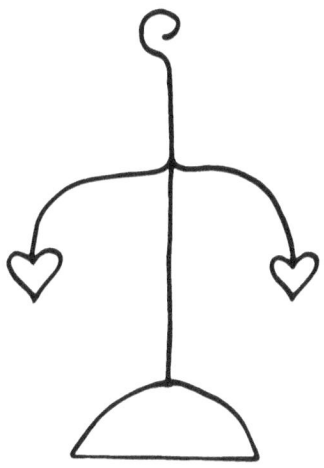

Everyone is equal before the law

In this world, we are really special beings, we should all already be aware of this. Who for one reason, who for another, after all, knows that he or she is special. However, I am not referring to a subjective characteristic, but to something objective. In fact, in our being there are different energies and three of them are capable of fully expressing themselves in the creation that surrounds us.

Let see which ones.

The *first* form of energy is clearly the most obvious to spot: it is the one that composes the body of which we are made. It is a form of energy that unites us with everything around us. In fact, the matter that constitutes our body is undoubtedly similar to what we can find in every other human being or in every other tangible thing belonging to the mineral, animal and vegetable world.

It is no coincidence that all these energies are similar: thanks to this fact our body is able to interact with them, nourishing, modifying and creating what surrounds it. As always, every coin has two sides and therefore the interaction is reciprocal and the body suffers the consequences.

The *second* energy that characterizes us, even if it is often taken for granted or overlooked, is obvious to all of us.

It is a hidden energy, a vibration, a music that no musical instrument can ever repeat. Unlike the previous energy, it is something unique in the world: there are no two equal ones.

Every individual is marked by a different energy. Even two homozygous twins, identical in all respects, differ in this aspect. This energy has different names, for example, life, soul or spirit. It doesn't matter which name you prefer to use, it's important to understand what we're referring to.

I have a habit of indicating as "voice" any vibration that I am able to recognize in creation, and I have baptized this type of energy as *Inborn Voice*. We have come into the world through and thanks to this vibration and our task, our purpose in life, is simply to bring it to fulfillment, to make it evolve to the highest perfection.

Of course, this same energy is clearly present in every other living being and even in what for us is something nonliving, for example a rock, a planet or a star.

The *third* energy we have at our disposal is the most magical: it is our voice, the very one we use every day to speak or sing. It is a very special energy, different from the previous two because we can use it at our discretion, behind a simple command, creating something that did not exist before, putting in vibration part of the existing matter, in the most usual case the molecules that make up the air.

This point is what makes us more aware that we are, in some way, similar to God, that we too are capable of creating something from silence.

The voice is the instrument that, practically, can allow us to bring our *Inborn Voice*, to manifest itself in the outside world. Obviously between saying and doing there is a beautiful sea. I would also say an ocean.

It is evident to everyone that simply pronouncing the word "chocolate", will not magically make it appear from nowhere in front of us. The fact that our voice is a suitable tool to bring magic to our world does not mean that it is enough to breathe life into the vocal cords to be able to do so.

To achieve this, even a little, you need to get in touch, align with your *Inborn Voice* and have at your disposal the right kind of material to put in vibration. If we succeed, can we consider ourselves equal to God? Maybe just a little. We must not forget that we carry only one *Inborn Voice* inside us, while our Creator possesses it all at the same time.

This idea is so old that its origin is lost in the dawn of time. Many legends and tales tell of powerful magicians capable of doing amazing things. Probably these are all fantasies, but you should keep in mind that every self-respecting magician, invented or not, has always had and used magic spells and words.

The idea of a magic word is clear to everyone, I don't need to explain it. Abracadabra, Hocus Pocus, Sim Sala Bim, Alakazam, Open Sesame, and Shazam are just a few of them.

Have you ever wondered what a spell is and what exactly spell means? A spell is *a state of enchantment caused by a magic word.* It won't surprise you to know that enchantment it is a word composed of the particle in and the verb to chant. Literally, it means to "sing inside".

Nice concept!

And what is the meaning of the word *sing*?

You will be even less surprised to know what it means: to *resonate*. So a spell is the ability to resonate inside.

This yes, that's pure magic!

One of the main reasons I chose to baptize the method I use to teach people how to use the voice to speak, socialize or sing, *Inborn Voice* is inspired by the halo of magic that surrounds the human voice.

Now that we have seen that everything is vibration and we have identified three energies that are certainly part of us, it is appropriate to begin to understand to which laws every vibration must comply with.

Unlike human laws, these laws are universal, which means that everything that exists or can exist is subjected to their respect. Nothing, nothing can escape them. Whether it's a sound wave, a brainwave, life or something even more intangible: every vibration is subject to the same identical laws.

These are laws that we can find hinted at or explained in different areas, even if not in the same terms or not related to the same topics.

It is not my intention to seek out whether their origin is divine or not. What is certain for me is that nothing and no one can avoid being subjected to these laws, not even those who created them. If God were to appear in flesh and blood among us, he could do no more than submit himself to the form these laws take in our world.

The laws that regulate the world are many, theoretically, there are twelve, but in our human condition it is already so much to be able to understand a couple of them.

We find the *first* law that regulates everything that can exist, in all the cultures of the world, from the oldest to the most modern, from religion to philosophy, and with good probability you have already encountered it sometimes in your life.

I call it the harmonic law because it serves to regulate the harmony, the balance, the center, of everything that exists. The law itself is very complex, not worth learning in its essence.

For our daily life it is sufficient to understand that everything that exists and is in a state of vibration is always and in any case subject to three distinct forces and that these always act simultaneously.

The origin of these forces is impossible for us to know, the important thing is to begin to understand that the forces that act in every single moment ever an energy, or vibration, are always and in any case three, never two.

Unfortunately, they taught us, from an early age, to always consider things on the basis of two points of view, a dualism. In black or white. Yes or no. Happy or sad. Rich or poor. As we grew up, we became so accustomed to this way of always breaking any idea or concept into two halves that we are now convinced that this alternation corresponds to reality. The reality, as you have all seen at least once in your life, is very different.

Probably few of you will have noticed the existence or the influence of this third force within our world. Some of you will have identified it only in the religious or spiritual sphere, for example the Christians believe in the Trinity of God, but not in everything that exists.

Everything that exists, every force that can modify the state of things, every energy can always be represented by three forces. The third force, despite passing unnoticed, is that which in reality is the master. It is so hidden in plain sight that no one seems to notice it, as if asleep.

Since it is important to understand the concept, I will give you some examples that can help you better understand the universal existence of this force.

Imagine you have a guitar in front of you.

If you have never seen one, imagine a rope stretched between two fixed ends, such as the line you may use to lay your laundry. Let us not complicate things and let us just consider one string. For this to start vibrating, some kind of external force is required to set it in motion, such as a pinch. The string, as such, has no force at its disposal. When you pinch the string of a guitar you give it an active force, that is, you give it part of your energy to vibrate with an undulatory way of "coming and going". If we pinch it pulling it upwards, when we let it go, it will begin to vibrate, first heading downward.

Our intervention on the string, our energy, is present only at the beginning. It is the tension that characterizes the very existence of the string, which leads it to develop a passive force, opposite to the previous one, which pushes it to rise again upward. This is a passive force because this type of energy is independent of any will. Neither we, nor the guitar, nor the string can do anything about it.

This is another universal law, that of resonance, that brings the string to vibrate in a continuous cycle of passive forces, alternating, in this case, upward movements with downward ones.

The common idea of many people is that there are only these two types of energy in our world. The first is active energy, or energy in which external intervention is needed for something to happen, and the other is passive energy, or energy that we cannot oppose to.

For example, if someone asks us a question we can answer "yes" or "no", acting as an active force. Vice versa, when it comes to asking a question, we can only accept the answer that will be given to us, whether it is a "yes" or a "no", so in this case, we are a passive force.

There is a third energy that is much stronger and more evident than the other two, but that no one considers. In fact, there is a force capable of neutralizing any active or passive energy, preventing it from continuing to express itself within the world. This energy is the same that causes the string to stop vibrating.

Science is able to give multiple explanations as to the cause that will stop the vibration of the string, for example the friction with the air or the transmission of the vibration to the structure that holds it. Surely the friction of the air affects the time when the rope stops, but even in the total vacuum, the rope will stop vibrating sooner or later. With an extremely long and thick rope the vibration might stop in a billion years, but at some point in the time it will stop inexorably.

Nothing is eternal.

The third force is the one capable of neutralizing any vibration.

The example I gave consider a string, so as we have seen before, a linear space with only one dimension. As the number of dimensions increases, it becomes too complex for me to expose, and I don't want to bore you anymore with very long explanations.

The important thing is to understand that this third force in our world is expressed in something that we might call a circular, or rather, spiral form. Not for nothing has science confirmed that there is a wonderful spiral in mathematics and nature. Some of these spirals are evident as in the shells of the snails or in the arrangement of the seeds of a sunflower on its corolla, while others are more difficult to detect at first glance.

In practice, the third force can be summed up in a cycle that repeats itself, that rises again, always identical to itself, if there is no continuous intervention of an adequate active energy.

This law helps us understand why everything in our lives tends to repeat itself. Yet few people notice it or they are aware of it. We resemble our parents, we always make the same choices, we tend to repeat the same mistakes, we always react in the same way.

The majority of people realize this cyclicality only for what they would like to remove from their lives, usually a vice or the repetition of some unwanted events. But even those who are more aware of it, tend to forget about it.

You will have already realized that you will not be able to change the way you act, not even by putting all the good will of the world into it. You may have tried every technique, every mode, every strategy. Yet, in the end, everything comes back and reappears.

Each of you may be aware of which vicious circle you are in, of which and how many attempts you have made to leave it behind. Yet the spiral continues to reappear every time, even stronger than before.

Sometimes you let yourself be subjugated by the cyclicality of events and stop resisting them. You simply don't care anymore.

I will try to give you another practical example of how these three forces are present and dominate our daily lives and our every choice. To be or not to be. Do or don't do. Right or wrong.

Imagine walking along a country road. When you took this route, you knew which destination was very important for you to reach, like the top of a sumptuous staircase, a riding stable of thoroughbred horses or a place to spend a holiday with serenity. As you walk down the street, the landscape start reminding you of something you have already seen, you even have the feeling of a dejà vu.

Continuing on, the landscape begins to become monotonous, always the same, until you totally lose all interest in looking at it. It will come, slowly, even to bore you to disgust and you can not wait for it to change.

At a certain point, you arrive at a fork in the shape of "T". The road you are on does not go any further and you can only choose whether to go left or right. From a practical point of view, there are no indications, so it is not important which way you choose because each of the two has the same chance of being the right one.

It's likely that when you get to the crossroads it's not even clear why you've got there.

This little story serves to confront you with

the duality that you somehow recognize exists in life. Anyone who is faced with a crossroads, immediately thinks they are faced with only two choices. Each one is potentially the right one, but it seems natural to stop for a moment to evaluate the situation before taking the chosen path.

If so far you have been able to recognize yourself in this story, I'm happy. This book will help you to understand how this crossroads is only a great illusion, a dream or, better said, a nightmare. Only your I*nborn Voice* can save you.

This illusion is probably the main reason why everything in life seems to be repeating itself forever.

The neutralizing energy is precisely the energy that you resonate with as you stop for a moment and decide which is the right way to continue.

This little hesitation participates in making the vibration decelerate the enthusiasm you had triggered at the beginning of the path, making it slow down or, better said, divert.

My working experience has led me to meet many people who have made a choice other than going left or right, demonstrating that there are never only two choices available.

For example, many people choose to stop right in the middle of the junction. I will say more: many of them even decide to sit down, even in positions that are not too comfortable, and wait for something to happen. Some are waiting for a traveling companion, others are waiting for the money to buy a vehicle, others are simply waiting.

Every day I also meet people who, tired of waiting, have even chosen to go back along the way, showing that the choices available were not two, but four!

These two additional choices are not immediately obvious to the inexperienced eye and are the practical effect of the neutralizing energy, which constantly attempts to oppose the creation of new energies.

In practice, if waiting means bending the way until it has a spiral shape, turning back means achieving the opposite result to the desired one.

An experience that many of us have felt over their own skin. You had gone down a path to get a promotion and you were fired. You had started the journey for getting married and you break up. You want to get in shape and instead you gain weight.

Some of you will easily identify with what I have said. Yet walking North, you should automatically leave the South behind, you should know.

If you stop injecting active energy northwards, perhaps wasting resources with pauses for reflection, sooner or later you lose the "straight" way and turn it into a big curve.

As I said, this triple nature of every energy has always been known, it is handed down in all the sacred texts and in all the cultures of the world. In Christianity it is explained as the triple nature of God and, even if other religions oppose the figure of Jesus, they keep the idea of a triple nature of our reality. The same idea can be found a bit everywhere, even if it has clearly been explained in more or less intricate ways than I just did.

Obviously, this first harmonic law is only one of many others that dominate creation. It is a law that helps us understand the life cycle of a vibration and how an active force is needed to maintain it alive.

The *second* law that I expose to you is the law of the octaves. It serves to understand how vibration propagates or evolves. It explains why a vibration is not able to express itself in a uniform and predictable way.

This law is not so mysterious. It has been known for a very long time, one could say it has always been. Given its name, many will have already guessed what I am referring to, indeed probably someone will also have a flourish on the subject, as it is something very similar to the mathematical law that is used to build the scale of current musical notes.

It is not my intention to talk about music theory in detail. This subject is widely debated in texts available to all and is remarkably complex to understand, both from a philosophical and from a mathematical point of view. Those of you who are more curious will surely be able to find satisfaction with the various texts of musical theory.

I refer to musical theory, specifically to the "octaves", but only to make you understand the abstract idea behind it. The reality of nature is very different and does not correspond to what is exposed in modern musical theories.

History reports that already in ancient times mathematics was used to produce musical instruments. They noticed that musical notes were perceived as harmonious only when they had certain proportional relationships with each other.

Obviously, at the time, there was no talk of frequencies, but everything was expressed in terms of the length of the strings set to vibrate.

For example, we find Pythagoras' studies on a tense string in which he demonstrated that by dividing a string according to certain mathematical relations, consonant sounds were easily obtained.

Regardless of the world of music, this law is universal. Whatever vibration exists is subject to this law.

Science has also empirically shown that by gradually increasing the frequency at which a string vibrates, its behavior is different from what one would expect. Technically speaking, its response is not "linear". There are times when the string tends to vibrate less than expected and others when it tends to vibrate more than expected.

From a practical point of view, unless you are a mathematician or a physicist, it is not necessary to know anything else.

When the vibration spreads along a string, resonance phenomena occur, naturally. Those who have dealt with the construction of musical instruments have somehow had to develop a mathematical system to avoid running into cacophonic resonance points. In fact, at those points, the musical notes become something unpleasant to listen to.

If the guitar strings had different proportions, plucking a note, it would not sound constant over time, but it would appear as "trembling".

The sound would not be constant in time because of the phases of acceleration and deceleration of the vibrations that would be caused by the phenomena of resonance.

All these examples are to give you a sense of something on a simple level so that you can move it to a more complex level. In fact, we do not live in the one-dimensional world of the string but in a much more complex multidimensional world. Yet these phenomena occur equally, albeit in a different way.

The important thing is to understand that in our world a vibration cannot evolve along a rectilinear trajectory, but tends to exist in what we could conceptualize as a spiral shape.

To make you better understand the concept try to imagine launching a boomerang. It is its shape, its very nature, that leads it to make a curved trajectory and return to the point of origin. The vibration "thrown" by a human being does a bit the same thing. It tends to behave like a boomerang, so at some point, it will find itself curving to perform a cycle to return to the origin.

In the world of music the notes of an octave are repeated every 12 semitones. In other words, a note, for example an A, as the frequency continues to rise, it first "becomes" B, then C, D, E, F and finally G. Continuing to rise in frequency returns to being an A. Clearly not the same A, but one belonging to the upper octave.

Imagining this concept in the world of a boomerang, it means that when it returns to its point of origin, it will no longer be in the hand of the person who launched it, but for example at his feet or beyond his head.

In practice, when an "octave" is raised, a vibration is taken to evolve, to move on to an upper level of the matter. Instead, when a vibration is lowered by an "octave", it is brought to a state of creation, on a lower level of matter.

Since we were not conceived as musical instruments with keys, built specifically to avoid these moments of slowing down or acceleration of vibrations, it is clear that every time we implement a vibration, it can not continue to exist always identical to itself and inevitably sooner or later will tend to return to the original state.

If we want to be able to control in some way this phenomenon, in order to bring to fruition our original intention, we must somehow continually act on the vibration that we have created.

To do this it is necessary to have some kind of tool, a guide, a compass, which allows us to understand when it is time to accelerate the vibration to avoid a slowing down phase, or vice versa, when it is necessary to let go of things because you are facing a phase of acceleration.

Without this instrument, we would find ourselves spinning empty, in a cycle that repeats itself forever.

We are special beings, essentially divine, because we have been created with this instrument, with this compass: our *Inborn Voice*.

5
THE HUMAN VOICE

Language has reduced voice to mere noise

What is meant by the word *voice*? The word *voice* is fascinating because its origins lie in the idea of giving things a name. Always to cite the sacred texts, within them we always find described that a superior being created all things, then brought an energy to lower its vibration to make it understandable to man, who then gave the name to everything talking or singing, thanks precisely to the voice.

It is important to understand that when I speak of voice, I am always referring to vibrations and not to words. Words are only one way of using voice, of channeling vibrations, but the two are absolutely distinct. In our world, there are about 7,000 different languages, so about 7,000 different ways to call the same thing, but it exists only one vibration that characterizes it.

The human voice is something unique in our world. You have certainly noticed that there are no other life forms on the planet that can speak. Of course, there are species that can perfectly repeat our words or the noises they hear, such as parrots and Indian blackbirds, just as there are other ways of communicating, such as the cries of alarm or the complex dances of the rituals of the mating of some birds. Ultimately, we are the only living species on this planet to have received the gift of the word, the ability to express to others what we live within ourselves.

Thanks to the collaborations and scientific research in which I participate, I am even able to highlight something that could surprise you: there are no significant anatomical differences between us and other primates.

This means that they have absolutely everything they need to talk. Yet they do not.

The main difference between us and the primates lies elsewhere, in our brains. It is, in fact, our brain that guarantees us the possibility of controlling with precision the movements of our phonatory apparatus, so as to be able to emit the different sounds in the right sequence and with the required speed.

It is always the brain that is solely responsible for our incredible ability to control breathing so that it is synchronized with the needs of speech.

Finally, it is always the brain that gives us the ability to understand and develop language. Considering these points, our uniqueness seems even more exciting.

For some reason, we have developed an entire area of our brain devoted to speech. Yet talking is not something necessary for survival, so much so that in case of extreme danger, none of us would ever dream of making a complex speech, but it is limited to screaming, just like all other forms of life.

The latest researches have confirmed what has long been suspected, that our ability to cry is instinctive and related to the oldest part of our brain. A newborn baby is very capable of crying from the first moment in which the air fills his lungs, without anyone having taught him anything.

Now that we know how lucky we are to have the gift of speech, it will be good to understand where this extraordinary ability is born.

Talking for us is something so common, so essential, that no one stops to consider that in reality, it is nothing instinctive, but it is something that we have learned to do over many years, with much commitment and effort.

My work often brings me into contact with deaf and dumb, blind or autistic people, so I don't need the help of science to understand where the human voice comes from.

The human voice is born in the ear, in close collaboration with the eyes. Unfortunately, those who are born deaf, if they do not receive help from the outside, they also remain totally silent, just as those who have some visual difficulties tend to emit sounds that are different from the norm or to communicate incorrectly.

Our voice, the unique characteristic that makes us so special, is actually a direct consequence of our five senses and the work of mirror neurons, all elements already available to us from birth.

I would like to point out a curiosity: current science has stopped at a Hamlet-like dilemma, in fact, it wants to establish whether the egg or the chicken was born first. It is trying to understand whether words are the origin or a consequence of our brain evolution. Obviously, we ordinary mortals are not interested in this kind of talk, at least not at the moment.

Participating in this kind of researches, albeit informally, has given me a lot of satisfaction, as well as receiving the recognition that my personal teaching method perfectly follows the natural systems of human learning.

To my knowledge, *Inborn Voice* is still the only method that teaches you how to use your voice as we are naturally predisposed to learn. All the other teaching methods, especially those involving the use of vocalizations and other sound-producing exercises accompanied by a piano, can actually be detrimental or even worse, harmful, as demonstrated by the many artists who develop nodules on their vocal chords or even worse problems that can be related to the inner aspect of the voice.

Human beings live at the same time in two very distinct realities. The first reality that we usually name "inner world", the one that only we can know, the second one is that of the outer physical world, that we share with everything else. Our voice is the means through which we put these two worlds into communication, so it is a kind of bridge of connection.

This ancestral and fascinating dualism is most probably at the origin of religions and spiritual disciplines. In fact, religion is a word that essentially wants to express the idea of putting together, of uniting different things: two worlds, two realities precisely. Among other things, I always like to tell people that many terms linked to the phonatory apparatus, especially the "medical" ones that I will omit, have something magical. The only common word related to the vocal apparatus it may help to outline now, without entering in too difficult Latin terms, is "jugular". This one, like others, are words that originate in the same Sanskrit root "Yug". This word, in Sanskrit originally expressed the idea of a means of conjunction or interaction with the divine.

So far we have spoken in more or less abstract terms, now I will try to go into more practical detail.

For simplicity, let's start by considering the part of the human voice that interfaces with the external world, even if this voice comes to exist long after our *Inborn Voice*, which as I already explained, begins to exist with us.

From the physiological point of view, science tells us that for each of us the learning of vocality takes place through identical mechanisms, even if it may follow a different path each time, essentially linked to "chance".

I will try to explain in the best way how the

human voice is born, to let you better understand how in reality everything is not so accidental.

All of us have begun to perceive sounds still in the maternal womb. At that stage, perception does not occur through the ear, but through the whole body, especially the bone structure.

Each of us perceived the outside world for the first time through the vibrations that resonated all around us and within our bodies.

This type of perception is not an exclusive ability of the pregnancy phase. Even today we are still able to perceive these vibrations through our bodies, even if we are not aware of them anymore. Our conscience chose not to pay attention anymore to these elements at an early age.

Today we could easily define this ability as our "sixth sense". In reality, it is still possible to activate this type of perception in different ways.

For example, it is very easy to listen to your body vibrate when you go to a concert or a disco and immerse yourself in music at high volume, but you can also do it in absolute silence.

With just a little effort of concentration,

during meditation, you may be able to perceive again the pulsing of our heart and listen to the flow of our blood inside the arteries and veins.

Once the ears are finally immersed in the air, they begin to pick up airborne vibrations for the first time. Imagine what emotion, what upheaval it may have meant to perceive for the first time all the sounds that surrounded us.

In those moments, each of us listened with our ears to our heart beating, to the sound of air entering our nose and filling our lungs, to the sound of our eyelids opening and closing, to the sound of our first feeds, to the sound of the caresses touching our skin.

Today all these sounds, for us, are part of the silence. Yet practically nothing has changed. It is our brain that has chosen not to pay attention to this type of stimulus anymore, but they still exist.

If you add to all this jungle of sounds the voices of people who sweet-talk babies, plus our own voices while crying or making noises, you can imagine the chaos that can be heard for the first time in the world. You may have a vague idea if you visit an open-air market in a foreign country where you don't know a word of the local language.

Scholars claim that it takes a newborn baby between 2 and 6 months to recognize their mother's voice through hearing. Yet we were all able to recognize our mother from the first contact, thanks to the perception of her heartbeat through our body.

It took each of us 7 to 9 months to recognize what sound was used to refer to us, our "name", so we could respond and give the first satisfactions to our parents. It took us almost a year to start associating some sounds with certain ideas or needs. As you can see, at this stage, the word is still far from existing.

Yet each of us, even those who have serious problems such as the deaf and dumb or the autistic, has cried and made noises from birth, bringing their inner vibration to resonate in this world.

Up until this moment, the ear was the undisputed master of our outer world, but little by little he gave up his scepter to the eyes that in the meantime "activated" themselves. Only when a child starts to associate a sound that he hears with an idea, thanks to the sense of sight, he can understand its symbolic meaning. Only at that moment does he realize that he is also able of emitting the same kind of sound and so begins to imitate those he hears.

On average it took us a year to start saying the first words, but at that stage of growth, they are just sounds and nothing more.

As we grew, through imitation and repetition, each of us was able to communicate in an increasingly complex way. Today it seems impossible, but it took about 6 years to start developing what we call language. And during these six years, little by little, without us realizing it, the scepter of the command has again passed from hand to hand.

Now it is the brain that owns it.

At the same time also our internal world grew, but it was quickly overwhelmed by the world of words. In fact when we now think, inside our heads, we find only words: we forgot what we were able to do before their advent.

The language used to communicate in the external world has simply evicted the one that already exists in our internal world. The same happens also to a 6-10 year old child who changes country: just a few years are enough to no longer speak his mother tongue, to forget it almost entirely.

To better understand this concept and how much language has invaded our lives, let's try for a moment to imagine waking up aboard an alien spaceship. Every attempt we make to communicate is null and void. They understand neither our language nor our gestures. And vice versa. We would find ourselves in conditions very similar to those present at the time of birth, with the disadvantage of being aware of the past and having less available all those evolutionary mechanisms that we used to learn to communicate the first time.

Of course, with a little willpower, in 4-12 months we would be able to learn to communicate again. Being isolated from other human beings for 3-10 years, we would forget our mother tongue. At some point, even our dreams and thoughts would exist only in the new alien language.

Another way to understand how much the language of the outside world has invaded us, actually replacing something primordial, is when we fail to remember a word or a name.

We have many ways to explain this type of discomfort, but in practice, our brain freezes while trying to find the missing word in its meanders.

We do not find peace until we remember the missing word and when we find it we are really happy. The brain knows no other way to identify what we want to name and remains as lost, leaving us with a bad feeling as well.

That bad feeling is linked to the little moment of awareness that takes us to listen, even if for a short moment, to our *Inborn Voice* that knows perfectly what is the "name", the vibration, corresponding to the word we are looking for.

As we have seen, our outer voice is shaped over many years. The mistake many people make is to consider their voice as something static and immutable. Practically every day I meet someone who tells me with resignation that he doesn't love his voice at all as if it were not possible to change this fact.

Those who realize that they do not love their own voice are to be considered lucky because they have the opportunity to recognize the existence of a dissonance between their outer voice and something more intimate and profound, namely their own *Inborn Voice*.

If you think about it for a moment, it is clear that when you express your taste in some area it is because you have some term of reference. I can say that I don't like something only when I have the opportunity to make a comparison with something else, which I know I like.

Many people are unaware of their voice and how they use it, but unconsciously they know perfectly if their voice is something they love or hate. Usually, those who do not appreciate their voice unconsciously, tend to highlight this fact speaking a little, in low voice or to speak a lot when there are noises or music around that make it difficult to listen.

This kind of attitude is comprehensible, if we do not like something, we tend not to use it, but clearly, it can only lead to sacrifices and missed opportunities.

Now that we have perhaps understood how language has evolved inside the external world, we can begin to consider the evolution that has taken place in our internal world. Understanding these steps will be more complex, but it is of fundamental importance.

As we have just seen, the development of language learned from the outside has completely replaced some other form of natural communication that previously existed within us. Today, when we think, we do it using the language we have learned from the outside world. Of course, somehow we have always been able to think, from an early age: we simply did not use the same methodology as now.

A small child who does not know the word "like", still has tastes and can refuse a certain type of food. The parent will think "he doesn't like it". The child simply expresses his or her disappointment with the means at his or her disposal, but within the child, there has been a process of communication, an argument. This form of inner thinking springs directly from our vital vibration, which is why I called it *Inborn Voice*.

At this point, you have to ask yourself: Has our *Inborn Voice* disappeared forever into thin air or does it still exist somewhere?

In order to understand the response, it is necessary to analyze its evolution.

When we are conceived, we are pure essence. At that moment our inner world is everything that exists and we know. Our consciousness is unlimited and is not linked to sensory organs or interaction with the outside world. Everything we need to survive is given to us without asking. We will carry on with this memory intact throughout our earthly life.

After the birth, everything starts to change.

You find yourself imprisoned in an alien body and world, of which you know nothing and of which you have to learn everything from scratch. All our knowledge is not able to express itself in the current state of our body and little by little, it is set aside, forgotten. Our *Inborn Voice* remains strong and present. It is characterized by an incredible desire to materialize in this world through every means at its disposal.

Gradually we grow up, generally surrounded by people who adore us and that after all, make us feel a bit like a deity. Our thinking is fluid and clear, free from narrow and incomplete ideas or words from outside, so it is unlimited.

When we start using our voice everyone seems very happy and loves us even more. Since our essence seeks nothing but love, it directs all its energies towards the development of language it finds in the outer world.

In doing so, it maintains its nature intact and in fact, in this phase of growth, the external voice is perfectly aligned with our *Inborn Voice*.

There are no filters or problems with its flow and in fact, it carries with it all the emotion that springs from within.

It is not for nothing that young children are always able to amaze, to excite and to give light to the truth of things.

They are not yet able to lie and are genuine.

In general, it is at this stage of growth that the first "error" occurs. Induced by the behavior of our parents and by their love, we take the first of many paths that will gradually distance us from our inborn ability to communicate.

The idea of going down the wrong path is something very appropriate because it is a mistake that is made in good faith. It is interesting to note that this idea has always been present in all ancient cultures and in the corresponding sacred texts, even if described in a different way.

You will be surprised to know that the word *sin*, used in so many religions, was originally a term linked to the idea of having made a mistake taking on the wrong path or on the wrong target. This first error, the "original sin" of many religions, the source of all the subsequent ones, is transmitted from generation to generation, precisely through the growth and weaning of their children.

What is this first mistake and when exactly is it that you start to create the separation between your *Inborn Voice* and your external voice?

When you start to learn to lie.

Lying is a word with an interesting meaning because it wants to express the concept of something unreal, invented by the mind.

For when you begin to lie, in jest or out of alleged necessity, you take a path that leads you right to become a chronic liar.

In the book I use the term lie in its strictest sense, I do not include any element of judgment or religiosity about it, I simply indicate the moment when someone puts into action an energy that is opposed to their *Inborn Voice*.

To lie in the first place is to give up the scepter of one's life to the mind, giving it the power to create energies and vibrations that are not reflected in the absolute truth of the internal world or in our perception of the external world.

In fact, the only truth that we can know as human beings is the one coming from within us, everything else we know is only the result of a sensory deduction, therefore a complicated and fascinating form of illusion.

For the moment, let's just consider the "lie" in terms of vibrations and resonances.

Let's try to better understand what a lie is. A lie is when you consider, speak or act for something that clashes strongly with our *Inborn Voice* or when you voluntarily choose not to listen to it. In practice, every time we deny the truth that we have within ourselves, we give life to a new vibration capable of creating something tangible in this world.

What we bring to creation is an alternative personality capable of splitting our essence into several parts. The essence knows the truth, the personality knows the lie. Our essence is not able to lie, while the mind that controls the voice has no problem in doing so.

Obviously, not all lies are able to split our essence, only those that we choose to carry on with us indefinitely, day after day, building on it a new identity of our own.

The more lies of this kind are created, the more personalities you can develop. If we think about it correctly, this kind of lie is what we do first and foremost to ourselves.

We lie to ourselves so well that sooner or later, we convince ourselves that the product of our invention corresponds to reality. At this point, we are no longer aware that we are just playing a part.

Each of us has begun to lie in an attempt to hide our essence from others, pretending to be someone else, perhaps for fear of not being suitable to give our love. Nobody, in the beginning, lies to receive love.

The problem is that the evolution of the personality at the expense of the essence also leads to distorting the meaning of love.

A newborn baby is always inclined to give love to others, a caress, an instinctively given kiss. Those who have developed a personality always tend to want to receive love, even when in reality they are convinced to give it to others.

When a newborn baby loves, he gives itself up and completely trusts its loved one. Growing up surrounded by "liars", he will probably learn that it is better to receive love than to give it.

Once he is an adult, for him loving means wanting another person all for himself, he will not give himself up and he will not trust the others even for a moment.

I would like to point out once again that in my vision lying is completely devoid of any element of judgment.

It is not necessary to consider all human beings and all their essences in the same way.

There will be those who came into this world to create and those who are here to destroy, those who evolve, those who devolve.

For example, if exist an essence destined to bring to creation things considered bad by the society, he will suffer tremendously if he forces himself to live as good and kind.

There may be the other side of the coin, which is some soul born to be good and kind who lives a life of hell because he had to behave in a reckless way to survive in his natural environment.

Those who think that we must all be kind and good, live in a world of fantasy, of lies, and are able to see only half of the existing vibrations.

If there is light, darkness must exist, otherwise, neither of us would be able to know and appreciate the difference between the two.

By lying to ourselves every day, we devote

much of our vital energy to sustaining and nurturing personalities, growing and developing them at the expense of our own essence which is neglected, as forgotten in a well-protected storeroom, usually for fear that it might make us aware of the truth.

The personalities mature and take over, while the essence remains in the infant state.

As we grew up, each of us forgot that we had listened with wonder to the beating of our hearts and had even heard the noise of the air filling our lungs. One forgets, like wrapped in a deep sleep, to have a vital vibration inside oneself and is convinced more and more that one is something different. The good news is that were we who lied to ourselves, so nothing is lost!

When I talk about essence and personality I'm not inventing anything new. Psychology is an art that studies precisely these aspects of human evolution, albeit from other points of view, with different expectations and very different objectives. Much of the problems that psychology deals with are called, not coincidentally, personality disorders.

I defined psychology as an art, even if it is classified as a science because I believe that it is a profession that requires the same qualities of sensitivity and attention typical of art forms.

I have collaborated and continue to collaborate with several PhDs on these very topics, thanks to my particular ability to detect the subtle vibrations present in the human voice. One of these researches started with the intention of studying the relationship between different narcotic substances and personality alterations. The study has shown that some psychotropic substances strengthen personalities, while others weaken them.

Researchers were surprised to find that, silencing all the personalities, what remains, appears to be a child of the age of 2-4 years very frightened and totally unsuitable for social relations. I was very happy to meet in person, in the outside world, what I call the *Inborn Voice*.

The funny part of this study and of all modern psychology is that they detect the presence of personality disorders when a person has only one dominant personality, completely inflexible, and is unable to change it to another depending on the surrounding events. According to science, in order for an individual to be healthy, he must project different personalities in different circumstances.

In my opinion, a healthy individual doesn't need personalities at all, he just needs to release his *Inborn Voice* to let it grow and develop.

It is clear that in our society, the evolution of our own *Inborn Voice* is something that is not considered at all and, in fact, it is extremely rare to find individuals who have been able to do so, albeit in a small part.

Each of us is potentially the "healthy" bearer of a profound dissonance between our vital vibration and our voice. In fact, due to resonance phenomena, the human voice tunes to its own personalities.

That is the main reason why many people I meet claim to have a "bad" voice or even to hate it. Somehow, these people are lucky. Not because I can help them to love their voice again, but because they are aware of some internal dissonance and try to give it peace.

Unfortunately, not everyone is so lucky.

On the contrary, some even forget that they have this aversion to their own voice, which they then subconsciously pass on to their children.

At this point, I want to point out that the *Inborn Voice* is something tangible in our inner world, and able to communicate and speak.

Each of us is certainly able to listen to it again in the noise that populates our inner world if just we want it. Being able to listen to one of the others is much more complex. In some way that I can't explain, I'm able to do it. This gift has been given to me and can be understood only by those who have a similar one. What I can do is to teach those who want to learn my method how to recognize when the *Inborn Voice* shines through in their everyday voice. You only have to learn not to listen to the words.

It is difficult for an everyday person to hear clearly the *Inborn Voice*, not because of a lack of good will or intelligence, but because it is something they have forgotten and have chosen not to listen to. I will try to let you understand this idea through some examples.

As you are reading this sentence, what happens in your inner world? You are making the words you read inside yourself speak in a voice without tone or color. You are creating a vibration inside yourself just like you would in the outside world.

This inner voice is not what I call *Inborn Voice*, but the voice of one of your personalities.

It is necessary to make some small efforts to find out which one it belongs to. Since the voices we normally hear in our inner world belong to the many personalities we have created, and since they are without tone and color, it is difficult to understand how many they are. Every personality has one!

Probably the one you are using now for reading these lines is your most curious personality or the one more interested in using the voice. Some lucky people are going to have their *Inborn Voice* read out. There is an easy way to recognize it within the inner world: it is the only one that has a tone and a color.

Another way to recognize it is to identify the emotions. The *Inborn Voice* is the only one that can make you excited, it's the one that makes you smile, cry, even while you read a book and think you've finally noticed the *Way of the Voice*. In fact, the *Inborn Voice* is the only voice capable of bringing emotions from the outside world to the inner world.

The reason why many people, when excited, can't find the words or the reason they're smiling or crying, is because they can't understand the language of their *Inborn Voice*. Communication took place on a different level from the normal one: you find yourself crying and you do not know why. There was simply a resonance with something, with a forgotten memory and very valuable for our *Inborn Voice*.

The reason why more and more people seem to become insensitive is the same: they have really closed their *Inborn Voice* so deeply that not even the emotions can reach it anymore.

The word "emotion" means bringing out what you have inside. In reality, it is possible to carry an emotion outwards even using as a filter one of the personalities we have developed.

The only trace of your *Inborn Voice's*

existence is when you keep silent and carry an emotion inwards.

Another way to understand the existence of the Inborn Voice may be to remember the last time you promised yourself something.

For example, a diet. How many times do we swear to ourselves that we should start a diet? We really do and one of our personalities is perfectly aware of this promise. It's a shame it isn't the same personality that goes out to dinner with friends, the one who goes shopping, the one who cooks or the one who sits eating.

Sometimes while we eat, the personality that decided to make the diet peeps out, and at that moment we realize that we are doing something contrary to our will.

Yet even then we are unable to stop eating.

The different personalities are fighting each other as if our body were a sort of machine managed by different automatic pilot. These little moments of lucidity are a symptom that you have inside of you something capable of observing, making you glimpse the reality but for some reason, it doesn't act: the *Inborn Voice*.

Once you understand the relationship between *Inborn Voice*, external voice and reality, it will be easier to understand why in my daily work I can achieve incredible successes just where so many others fail.

Just to make people understand how different my approach is from the usual one, I can tell you that when I help children with problems related to communication, even like autism, I work on the communication skills and the voice of the parents, not directly with the children. In my experience, people with autism can communicate much better at the *Inborn Voice* level. By helping parents develop theirs, they will be able to communicate and help their children.

To make a comparison, the vibration produced by a person's normal voice is similar to the one of a musical instrument. If we were to analyze it from a scientific point of view, we would be able to describe it perfectly and completely. Nothing would be dispersed.

Instead, those who use their voice in perfect alignment with their *Inborn Voice* can create vibrations also within unconventional matter, resonating also inside planes that go beyond those measurable by science.

    The way I like to describe this phenomenon is as if a simple musical note produced with our *Inborn Voice* contains an entire "octave".

6

ONE, NONE, OR ONE HUNDRED THOUSAND?

*Words regret the time
when they were pure vibration*

So far we have made a journey that has accompanied us through the different stages of evolution of energy, starting from the purest, the one that distinguishes us and makes us unique, our *Inborn Voice*. We also already considered the voice we use to speak and sing every day, so all we have to do now is understand the relationship between the voice we use and the words we speak.

It is important to understand that voice and word are two distinctly different things. In fact, the voice exists independently of words and does not even need words to communicate (for example, a scream). This is mutual because words exist independently of the voice and do not need the voice to communicate (e.g. those written on this page).

Our human voice can express the same idea using different words within the same language or it can even choose to use a different one, for example a local dialect, French or even a dead language like Latin.

The *Inborn Voice*, as you probably have already guessed, does not use words at all.

Words are a creation of this world.

The *Inborn Voice* communicates through a superior and perfect "language", made of only vibrations.

It is not something that can be described using a language, not even a technical one like, for example, music. It's like listening to a wonderful melody in which each note contains a whole melody or an entire "octave".

We have already seen previously why the *Inborn Voice* does not know how to express itself using words: it is not able to lie and everything it expresses is a universal truth. A word, even one chosen with great care and attention, will never be a container large enough to be able to describe a truth in its entirety, but only a partial representation, linked to a precise moment.

Time is another feature that differentiates the two voices. The *Inborn Voice* cannot refer to the past or the future, since it exists in a dimension where time, as we know it, does not exist. If we think about it for a moment, it is also clear to us that every time we talk about past or future events, our memory or our imagination leads us to fill in missing spaces or to invent things that do not correspond at all to reality.

Understanding this passage is fundamental because it allows us to better understand the mechanism by which many disciplines of personal growth, ancient or modern, are able to show to those who approach them in a moment of spiritual awakening, a fascinating veil of truth capable of lulling them back to a new illusion that gradually will make them sleeping again.

All these disciplines have reached us in some adventurous way and in an incomplete form just because those who transmitted them, or those who received them, have used a form of communication unsuitable for the purpose: they have used words.

Pure knowledge is something that each one of us possesses in our own depths. It can be achieved, one can draw on it, but it is not something that one can control with the intellect or express with words.

When we come into contact in the external world with a part of the truth that we have always known from our inner world, we are fascinated and trapped like in a spider's web.

Only the *Inborn Voice* can transmit this type of knowledge intact, between two individuals who know how to communicate on this level and are able to do so without being confused by other vibrations. If you persist in using words, considering them for what they are, you can do no more than "lie" to yourself, addressing your energy in the wrong direction. Using words our energies are directed towards the creation of something, but not what we may think. It only creates a complex illusion that something is actually happening in the reality.

When we approach these types of disciplines we risk developing an additional personality capable of muting the trill of our essence that had miraculously managed to make itself heard, bringing us back for a brief moment to inner awareness.

As I explained earlier, personalities consume virtually all of the vital energy we have. Some of the personalities created under the illusion of having found something "superior" are so demanding of energy that they force us to try to feed them by absorbing the vital energy of the people we meet every day. In fact, it is not uncommon to meet homogeneous groups of people who share these personalities. They are convinced to support each other, but in reality they are simply feeding the dominant personality with their energy. A sort of "energy vampire".

Let's go back to see how words and language are something useful and necessary.

The main illusion of the human being is that language is something that can transmit information between individuals in a clear and understandable way. I did not choose the word "transmit" by accident. In fact, it is a term that has been associated with the transmissions related to electromagnetic waves, such as radio, television, telephone and so on. Transmitting a vibration is technically possible, just as you can receive it elsewhere, intact.

Even the term "individual" was not picked by accident. The word *individual* indicates the idea of something that cannot be divided without losing its essence. In fact, every human being is characterized by different personalities that are impossible to split without dispersing its essence. As we have seen before, a personality is something that each of us creates on the basis of one or more stimuli, to keep our essence hidden from the outside world.

When our essence wants to communicate with the outside world, or when we want to get in touch with it, we need to take back the voice and language that was born with us: vibration.

It is fundamental to understand that a vibration cannot and must not be filtered or created by a personality, otherwise it is like speaking in English with a someone that only speak Japanese, where even the gestures made with the head may have different meanings.

I'll try to make you understand these concepts by making a parallel in the world of music and music recordings that I know quite well. I guess everyone has had an experience, even a minimal one, of listening to a piece of music or a singer's voice from a recording.

Let's imagine we are alone in a huge and totally dark room, in the company of a violinist who plays for us. The sound waves produced by the musical instrument reach our ears practically intact. This is a type of communication composed only of vibrations.

If we want to record the violinist, we must first use a microphone. Each microphone has been built with certain technical features that allow it to transform the sound wave into an electrical signal. Changing the type of microphone would also forever change the electrical signal produced.

Then the electrical signal coming from the microphone is sent to an amplifier capable of transforming it once again, making it electrically more intense. Each amplifier, like the microphone, is built with certain technical characteristics, so changing the type of amplifier, would forever change even the amplified signal.

Then the output of the amplifier is then inserted into a mixer, which equalizes the electrical signal according to the technical characteristics with which it was built and according to the settings chosen by the taste and experience of the person using it. In this case, changing the mixer or its settings will radically change the result.

Now comes the last step where the output signal from the mixer is finally recorded on some kind of suitable media. Once again, depending on the type of technology and the type of substrate, the result will change enormously.

With this whole sequence of operations,

complicated and technological, we have reached only halfway through the communication process, as we have only prepared one of the countless recordings that we could have made by changing any of the variables in the technical process. For the communication process to be complete, someone needs to listen to the recording.

To listen to the recording you will have to follow the reverse procedure. The information present in the recording, which as you have already guessed is already radically different from what the violinist played, will be altered again by a process of amplification, mixing and reproduction by the speakers, creating a sound wave, a vibration, this too strictly dependent on the playback system and the settings of those who use it.

The resulting sound has nothing to do with the original one produced by the violin, it doesn't even sound like the original, even if it might seem so to the ears of an ordinary person.

I'm not the only one who argues for that idea. Science also says so, but there are many people who are able to tell the difference. A violinist, or other people with trained ears, can immediately recognize the difference between a recording and an instrument. Hi-fi enthusiasts can even recognize which amplifier or speakers have been used to generate the sound, demonstrating that the original vibration has been disrupted by the communication process that leaves a mark and in a way that is still identifiable.

Up to now, we have assumed a type of recording that is "ancient", based exclusively on vibrations. After the year 1990, the entire music world was disrupted by the introduction of digital technology.

We can compare this advent with the creation of a language. Making digital, in the field of music, essentially means taking a musical wave, analyzing it in certain and precise moments of time and converting it into a number based on choices of opportunities and predetermined rules. These choices actually destroy the 99.9% of the information present in the original recording.

High-fidelity enthusiasts and musicians are

able to recognize whether the recording of the violin took place on an analog medium, based on vibrations, or digital, based on a numerical language. I don't need to suggest that digital music is considered an abomination by many music lovers. As it is easy to guess, there is a deep split between the identity of the original sound wave and the final one.

A language may be able to transmit intact only objective information coming from the external world and not subjective information coming from the internal world.

To my knowledge, the only language that currently exists that is able to transmit information between two or more individuals intact, without this being distorted in any way, is mathematics. In fact, mathematics is based on the observation of objective facts that cannot be interpreted. Once you have learned a minimum part of the mathematical language, anyone is able to understand what a mathematical formula or geometric form is. For example, there is no doubt about what "1+1=" means or how to tell a triangle from a rectangle.

Even music, an art form that springs directly from our inner world, is a subjective language. In fact, only the notes, the pauses, the intentions are written on the score, but each artist takes his own when he plays or sings a piece of music.

The problem of the practical impossibility of communication between two individuals has always been known, so much so that this subject has also been dealt with in ancient texts. An example of this is the story of the Tower of Babel, in which the introduction of language had led men to no longer understand each other. We must not give credit to those who propose the creation of a new language as a solution, because nothing would change.

The words we use every day can only be useful when we try to communicate something objective and clearly perceivable through our senses.

Unfortunately, it is impossible to describe something subjective in objective terms, for example using a mathematical language, because the resulting mathematical formula would contain something based on a term impossible to determine: the subject trying to express the idea.

The split between your *Inborn Voice* and your everyday voice began with language learning. Unconsciously we all thought it was an unmistakable method of communication and all the decisions we took later, including the creation of our different personalities, are a direct consequence of words.

Once we get into the language, everything becomes full of erroneous suppositions, of words misused and of non-existent classifications. Since our adult thinking structures are built over language, then our thinking also suffers from the same problems.

How many meanings can a single word have? One, none or a hundred thousand?

Each word can have as many meanings as the people who listen to it or read it, to which we must add the one who used it. Our language is something extremely subjective and very few people are aware that they use the same identical word to express things that are actually very different from each other.

The sooner we realize that every verbal communication is inaccurate, or if we want to use my own terminology, is a "lie", the sooner we can set out on the *way of the voice* and begin to understand ourselves and all our loved ones.

Even now, as you read these pages, you are thinking about understanding the message that I wanted to convey to you. Yet this might not be the case. The implications of what I am trying to put on paper goes far beyond the capabilities of the human being, let alone those of written language.

As we have already seen, we use terms every day that implies the idea of the existence of communication based on vibrations. One of these fascinating examples is the expression "according to" (i.e. being in harmony with).

How many times have we been in disagreement with someone, spending hours of our time trying to make them understand our point of view, and then discovering that we were actually talking about the same thing?

Or how many times have we left a meeting convinced to have made the perfect argument and then discovered that in reality everyone had understood something different?

Let us try to understand this by means of a few examples. Each of us uses words that only appear to be identical but in reality they have a totally different meaning inside our inner world.

Let's take the word "mother" as an example and see how many different meanings we can find for this omnipresent word. The word *mother* has a different meaning for each of us. Many of us will identify this word with the female person who gave birth to us, the adopted with the one who raised them. Here, too, there is a deep split in the meaning we give to the first word we say.

At an early age many of us are led to think that all mothers are equal, then growing up we begin to understand that there are differences, even substantial, between the way of being a mother for various women.

Some people identify the word *mother* with those who spiritually guide them, be it a Guru, the Virgin Mary or some other important figure.

Other people identify the word *mother* not with a person, but with memories, for example with their favorite dish cooked by her, with a photograph placed next to the bed, with a story told to their children.

Within each of us there are one hundred thousand meanings for the word *mother*, depending on the context in which it is used or the idea we have in our hearts at a given time.

Of course, it is possible to be more specific by adding many other words next to the word *mother*, but the added precision is only an illusion because each word added to the sentence does nothing but greatly amplify the inaccuracy of each idea as you can not know, or even imagine, what can be found in the experience of those who receive the message.

Let us now take the word "car".

Probably many of us have a car. When we use it in one sentence, we are all talking about a different car. Yet the word is the same. There is more. Some people will use the word *car* to indicate something that is not even a personal motor vehicle, perhaps a railway carriage or a chariot. As you can see, a word, countless meanings.

Another useful way to understand how inappropriate our language is to express something subjective can be to consider words that in our daily life have little importance for us.

Take for example the word "snow" or "ice". Almost all common languages use only these two words to define two different type of water states. I traveled a lot and discovered that the people of the colder regions, since their survival was linked to a perfect understanding of what kind of snow or ice they met, developed more specific words. For example, there are those who use five words to define snow and seven words to define ice. There are even languages that have no words to define snow or ice because they had never seen its existence in ancient times.

The same applies to colors. Some primitive populations that I had met, within their language do not even have words to differentiate between colors. They use only terms that we could make correspond to "light" or "dark". Generally, the first color that appears in language as a word in itself is red, the color of mammals blood.

When a person in our society has to indicate the color of a newborn chick, what can he do?

It may just say that the chick is yellow. He can specify that it is chick yellow, canary yellow or lemon yellow, but he has no way of knowing if the other person has ever seen a live chick, as well as a canary bird or a lemon. This uncertainty happens even if the other person has seen the same chick as us, but at a different time. In order to be perfectly in agreement about the color, it would be necessary to see the same chick, in the same instant and from the same point of view. This may not yet be enough because we are not given to know if the other party has any visual defect, such as color blindness.

Taking this thought to extremes there is no possible way to know with certainty whether each of us perceives the same color in the same way. If two people observe the same color at the same time, they are clearly able to identify the color in the outside world, but nothing and no one can ever guarantee that the color they observe in their inner world is identical to that of the other. If a person could take a peek directly into the subjective world of another person would realize that they find nothing of what they think they know, everything would appear new and incomprehensible.

An intuitive way to understand how deep the language of words is in our being is to try to remember a song. Very few people are able to separate the words of a song from its music and treat them as two separate things.

Many times when you try to remember a song you think about its words. Sometimes words return to the mind without music, leaving you with that feeling of having the chorus on the tip of our tongue and until you remember it exactly you stay "in a limbo".

Other times you listen to musical notes and you have a "déjà vu". You start searching in your mind, again for words, to identify where you had already heard the same notes, perhaps assuming a plagiarism.

For example, ask yourself to remember only the musical motif, the notes and not the words, of the song "Old MacDonald had a Farm". Are you able to detach the musical notes from the words?

Words are not suitable containers to transmit subjective ideas between individuals, however they are suitable to intuit some aspects of the personality that is using them, and therefore of the essence that is kept hidden in the shadow.

In many cases, but not always, there is a deep relationship between the identity of an individual and some of the words that he or she chooses to use or that he or she chooses to oppose with great energy.

Many times, especially in the artistic or working field, people choose to use an artist name, a nickname or a title as a means of identification. Sometimes this nickname is not used verbally, but only in written form, for example to create an e-mail address or some other type of technological identification. Since there are no accidents, it is of little importance to trace the origin of this nickname, the important thing is to understand if somehow a part of us recognizes ourselves in that nickname.

Generally the chosen nickname, almost by magic, reflects in full what our essence considers to be its main defect, what it wants to keep hidden and for which it has built the personality that today is dominant. In some countries, nicknames are so popular that people use them even on business cards.

Originally the task of the personality was only to keep hidden some aspect of our essence, but since keeping a personality alive requires the use of many of our available energies, this choice will only set in motion vibrations, which will gradually make come true just what you wanted to avoid.

If the essence could decide to otherwise invest the same energies it devotes to nourish the personalities, it could easily change its destiny and guarantee its evolution.

The words that seem to be missing from the personal dictionary are just as interesting.

In this case, it is easier to recognize the lack of a few words in other people's vocabulary and it is more complex to realize one's own shortcomings.

Everyone happens to hear or repeat phrases such as "you didn't ask politely", "you are not able to apologize", "you never tell me I love you" or "you do not listen to me". It really seems that some people are resistant to pronouncing certain words, especially when they are explicitly asked to do so.

Somehow these words are directly connected with some deep emotion, part of their essence, and even using them annoys the dominant personality. It is not an inability to use certain words, in fact in other moments, perhaps more intimate or more social, in which another personality temporarily becomes dominant, is possible to see the same person using them fluently. This generally upset those who have so long expected to hear those words from them.

Finally, there are people who get really emotional, almost as if their lives were at stake, when they are confronted with certain words. They almost seem to explode and want at all costs to convince everyone that the idea represented by that particular word is the absolute evil. The more they spend their energies fighting against that word or what it represents for them, the more they become aggressive.

ONE, NONE, OR ONE HUNDRED THOUSAND?

Each of us knows someone who warms up instantly when dealing with a topic or an idea that can often be summed up in a single and simple word. In my work, I have met people who are hurling themselves up against those who have qualifications, people who show a deep hatred for those who have a different kind of sexuality and people who have a very bad relationship with money. And many of them have no apparent reason to get so warm, except wanting to hide even more deeply part of their essence that resonates with that idea.

So far, I have given a few examples with individual words, but exist also what I call the "greenhouse" language.

The idea of the greenhouse is that of a closed structure, dedicated to the cultivation or shelter of plant species in need of protection from the elements. The greenhouse language proposes the same concept: someone with a personality greedy of energies begins to gather followers to absorb part of their one. In order to protect its little garden, it develops a language that all members adopt unconsciously and each time they use those words they voluntarily release their energies to the greenhouse keeper.

These people are easily recognizable by the use of particular terms to describe otherwise very usual things. It is not uncommon to find groups of people, from school age on, who tend to identify and recognize themselves through a particular "language".

So far, I have poured out a torrent of words in a difficult attempt to explain something profound.

It is time to leave some room for silence.

The greatest fear of any human being is silence, yet there are cases when people choose to just remain silent. For example, when you feel guilty, when you are at fault, when you are caught by surprise or by something unexpected, you remain silent. You remain silent because you do not have any personality to oppose the event and you do not know what to say or do. In general, your eyes are also lowered and you remain motionless.

In those moments, with a minimum of awareness, you will be able to glimpse your own *Inborn Voice*. Slowly, if these moments are repeated over time, everyone will manage to develop a defensive personality to use against the silence, and this opportunity is lost.

When you encounter one of these situations you have an incredible opportunity to really know who is in front of you. It takes very little to tune into your *Inborn Voice* and start a vibration-only dialogue. Unfortunately, when these situations occur, one person remains silent, while the other tends to hurry at him and take over.

Another moment of silence, surely less welcome, is disease. As I am very open minded, I have participated in some studies with the terminally ill. In fact, doctors noticed that their patients stopped talking once aware of the terminal disease. They do not have ready a personality to oppose at the disease and their dominant one understands that its presence has become useless and stop acting.

At this point, I would like to clarify my concept of silence. The silence I am talking about is not marked by the absence of words or of what is called an internal dialogue. I often meet clients who practice some form of meditation and are convinced that they can achieve "inner silence". They have actually been very good at developing a new personality that manages the illusion of this new state very well.

Silence cannot be induced or controlled by the head. The mind creates only illusions. Actually, the *Silence*, the one with the capital "S" to which I always refer, is full of music, vibrations, something that is part of us and is not at all "devoid of sounds". As I explained in chapter three, it is a deafening silence.

You need a good dose of awareness to recognize your *Inborn Voice* by yourself. To be able to unhinge the personality that protects it, it will be necessary to walk along *the way of the voice* and then go through it all, until the end.

Freedom is something you only get if you choose to rid yourself of all the personalities you have created to protect our essence.

7
THE TWELVE ENERGIES

*Walking without the right guide
is like asking to get lost*

Our body has evolved to become a perfect machine capable of achieving great results in the quite hostile planet that generated us. All our evolution, in extreme synthesis, can be summarized with the idea of obtaining the maximum yield with the minimum expense.

Thanks to this evolutionary strategy we have been able to shape, little by little, the entire planet. When we find ourselves in situations where there is a real scarcity of resources or great difficulties to overcome that threaten our survival, this type of strategy has undoubtedly proved to be the winning one. Without it we would never have reached where we are today.

At our present stage, this same strategy is proving to be a real obstacle. On the one hand, we are destroying our planet in order to accumulate goods that are no longer necessary; on the other hand, we are not able to trigger our next evolutionary step. Unconsciously, we always implement solutions that aim more to save the vital energies of the individual than to achieve outstanding results.

Now that we seem to be in a time of abundance and goods are no longer scarce, it no longer makes sense to save vital energy, on the contrary, it is better to invest it to obtain results of a very different depth. Evolution has led us to be a perfect machine, but which has almost forgotten how to create vital energy. And when it luckily accumulates enough energy, it no longer knows how to save it for when it is required.

At this point you should have understood that when I speak of energy I am referring to the purest sense of the term: vibrations. To better understand this aspect, let's analyze together the structure of the "human" machine from the energy point of view.

Every human being is obviously born endowed with a body, more or less perfect according to the canons of our society. The body, as we have seen, is the manifestation of some form of very common energy around us.

Each of us is capable of understanding the difference between a living being and a dead one. Whether an insect, an animal or a human being, we are all able to determine when life is present and when it is absent.

We have previously seen how life is a form of energy, very rare and precious. It is not just any form of energy, but energy of the purest kind that we are given at birth.

We can safely say that these two types of

energy, the one that makes up the body and the one that keeps us alive, are also present in all that we recognize to be "living", such as animals or plants. On the contrary, it will be more difficult to understand their presence even in what we do not recognize as being "alive".

These two types of energy, vibrations, go to the extremes of our earthly existence.

On the one hand we have the vital energy, capable of vibrating at such high frequencies that it is impossible to measure or perceive it in this world; on the other hand we have the material energy, capable of vibrating at a much lower frequency and which science is beginning to define more clearly only in this historical age.

Every vibration when it "lives" inside an object always creates phenomena that are described by science as "resonance".

Resonance happens when the vibration tends to accelerate or decrease inside the object, at some specific points. To better understand the idea of resonance, imagine dropping a coin into a small container full of water, such as a bowl. Waves that branch off from the initial point of impact naturally head towards the edges. Each wave, arriving at the edge, will "bounce" and go back, creating a web of overlapping waves that soon turns into chaos.

When two waves meet, they somehow add up to each other, temporarily creating a third wave, larger and more powerful than the individual ones. Observing the ripples of the water in slow motion it would be really easy to notice these "points" of resonance.

It is interesting to note that resonance is a completely natural phenomenon, which cannot be reproduced artificially: you can't force anything or anyone to resonate!

For this to happen, of course, it takes an incredible coincidence of events, but these are surprisingly frequent. For example, television, radio, mobile phone and WiFi only work thanks to resonance phenomena.

Our perception of lights, sounds, smells and whatever else is due to these phenomena.

Even sperm fertilization of the egg takes place through resonance. Of the millions of spermatozoa that try to get inside the egg cell, only one, and only one, has "by accident" the appropriate resonance frequency to get inside. All the others are excluded because they don't have the right frequency.

Of course, also our body resonates and within it, our *Inborn Voice*, naturally creates resonance points and creates frequencies that can be more or less easily identified. Applying a same source of vibration to the same body, these points will always be the same: changing body or changing the vibration, everything will move elsewhere.

The *Inborn Voice* is something unique, special, that each of us has since birth. It is wonderful that there are not two human beings in the world who have identical energy. Like the physiognomy, fingerprints and many other elements that characterize us, each of us is endowed with a unique vibration.

Now I will try to help you understand how this vibration can come into contact, or rather in resonance, with our physical body and with much of the matter existing on our planet (and in the universe).

THE TWELVE ENERGIES

Given the enormous speed with which this type of energy vibrates, it is evident that in order to be able to interact and resonate within our body and the rest of creation it must undergo different stages of slowing down. Every oriental discipline tries to explain these concepts in a more or less clear way, for example using names such as *chakras* or *bodies*, but unfortunately what has come to us has been handed down and interpreted in a too free or absolutist way.

The two main mistakes that most of the existing ideas have in common are to consider man as something complete already at the moment of birth and to imagine every human being as similar as others.

Some of these theories even go so far as to want to identify the exact point in the human body where a particular form of energy would manifest, or to define its corresponding color or musical note.

In my experience, all this is something so far from reality that it is better to forget it.

Those who support these things forget that colors and musical notes are a convention created by the human mind: they are something that does not exist in nature.

In fact, in nature there is no sound, not even in birds singing, that is perfectly corresponding to the musical notes we use today. I will tell you more. In ancient times musical notes were different from modern ones and many ancient musical instruments, including my beloved Stradivari violin, were not designed to produce them. To "stretch" and "tune" a Stradivari violin to modern notes, you even need to reinforce it to prevent it from literally breaking apart.

The same applies to colors. We forget that if we observe, for example a chick and this appears yellow to us, it is because its feathers do not absorb the yellow vibration of white light. What appears to us to be yellow is actually not yellow at all, but it's complementary color instead!

Much better to try to reconstruct one's own theory from the beginning, so I will try, as far as possible, not to use the same terms already used by others, so as to facilitate understanding by those who have already made those ideas their own.

Let's try to reconstruct together a logical and deductive path to identify the different level of steps that the *Inborn Voice* makes lower its energy level, or rather, when it goes down in "octave", to bring the matter that makes up the human body to a state of creation.

The main forms of life we know are divided between the animal and plant worlds. This scientific division helps us to immediately identify the fact that we and the animals are able to move and interact with the world in a way that is certainly superior to that of plants and minerals.

As we have learned in the first pages of the book, every force that expresses a tangible result in this world is certainly a force, an energy, a vibration. So here we have identified a third energy, a first resonance of our *Inborn Voice*: the ability to move.

It is very interesting to note how words play tricks to us. The word *animal*, includes within it the Latin word "anima", the idea of *soul*, so there is no doubt that the original meaning of whatever we conceive as a "soul" should be part of their existence too. The religious discussions that often take place on this topic are mostly due to the meaning that is given to the word *soul*. In fact, the profound meaning of the soul is "vital breath", but in my vision, the soul is only a resonance produced by the *Inborn Voice*, the energy that allows us to animate, or to move as we like.

Another characteristic that is our own and that is linked to our existence is the ability to feel, generate and share emotions. Even emotions are definitely a vibration, a form of energy.

Who better than us can recognize their existence in our inner world and can appreciate the more or less pleasant effects they trigger?

There is no doubt that emotions are a second type of resonance of our *Inborn Voice*, a fourth type of energy that sets us apart.

To sum up, we have seen that the particular energy that distinguishes each of us, the *Inborn Voice*, is manifested in this world by going down by "octave" (or if you like by frequency), to give shape to the body. During the descending path it passes through several "octaves" and each time generates, through resonance, some form of characteristic energy capable of manifesting itself in this world.

So far we have identified the energies that give us the possibility to move and the possibility to feel emotions. These four forms of energy (*Inborn Voice*, Body, Soul, and Emotions) are typically present in each of us from birth.

Of course, there are others energies.

The other forms of vibration, contrary to the most widespread belief, are not available immediately but must be cultivated and strengthened in some way. A human being is perfectly capable of completing his entire life cycle only with these four forces, the others are not at all indispensable and I even say that very few feel the need or the possible lack of them.

The fifth form of energy, the first that most humans develop is our voice. As we have seen this form of energy is very particular because it is easily available and allows us to vibrate part of the matter that surrounds us in a way clearly perceivable with our senses. During the first years, as a baby, we use our voice in a more instinctive and graceful way, for example to signal states of need or to make some emotion flow, then growing up everything becomes more controlled and less "natural".

Given the tangible appearance of this energy, it is possible to appreciate how it manifests itself in a unique and particular way, more or less present, in each of us.

As we grow we begin to develop the organ that best characterizes us as a human species: our prodigious brain. The energy of the mind is something that reaches maturity in much more time than the voice. It is possible to indicate more or less a first "start" of this energy around the age of 10 years. This sixth type of energy is usually the one that over time dominates, more or less totally, the previous five.

The last type of energy that normally develops in every human being is sexual energy. It comes to manifest itself in its entirety with puberty and generally, its advent causes quite a few shocks and it takes some time to be able to learn to live peacefully with it.

If you have counted correctly, we already

have seven different types of energy within our small "factory". As we have seen, the first four types of energy are available for everyone, and the last three must be developed and brought to maturity.

One thing is knowing how to use a form of energy, another is mastering it. In fact, although talking, thinking and reproducing are not difficult for anyone, mastering these energies is something truly complex.

The human being is able to become a great man or woman and live a perfectly healthy and happy life without any other kind of energy.

In my working field, that of voice, I can affirm that very few people are able to effectively use their voice as it was meant by nature. Voice is an instrument that, at the very least, must be able to let the other vibrations present inside us, such as will and emotions, shine through.

Yet very few people manage to do it.

Every day I teach people to reconnect their emotions and thoughts to their own voice. Many of them have extreme difficulty in relating to other forms of energy, especially their own emotions. And if there are few people who are able to superimpose the vibrations of emotions and will on those of the voice, those who can make something of the enormous power included in our voice are extremely rare.

For the moment I will stop with these seven types of energy, the most classic and useful to understand the next steps.

In all, a human being at the peak of his development is able to manage and convey as many as twelve different types of energy.

It would be useless to expose the last five as they become accessible only when in contact with your *Inborn Voice* and it really takes a lot of time, sacrifice and passion just beginning to perceive their presence.

If you compare this exposition of mine to the classical ones, you will find some common points and some differences.

The main difference, as I said, is that some vibrations of the "classical" conception are not granted to every human being. In fact, those who exhibited and handed down these theories had before them an uncommon being, probably endowed with all twelve energies. The other difference is that they want to identify "energy" points in specific areas of the body.

In the best case, the points that have been "codified" are those where the energy is more simply identifiable, or where it is present at the minimum of its full power.

I will try to give a simple explanation of this concept. If we were faced with a "perfect being", gifted and in control of all the forms of energy at his disposal, and we had the ability to perceive his vibrations, we might notice the presence of some points where the energy appears more static, therefore more easily recognizable.

Let's take the usual example of a guitar string. If we could observe it vibrate in slow motion, we would notice that within the movement there are points where it appears almost motionless. These are not the resonance points, but those that immediately stand out to the eye because they appear static. In fact, at those points, the vibration has the lowest possible energy level.

To understand what a resonance point is, it is necessary to observe an object in vibration, for example the classic crystal glass, that will at some point explode subjected to the vibrations of a sound. Observing the glass in slow motion, we would see that the rim begins to shatter, not at the points where the glass vibrates less, but at those where the vibration goes beyond the elastic capacity of the crystal. Each successive sound wave, because of the resonance, is added to the previous one, transforming what would be an imperceptible movement into something destructive.

That is why ancient representations of energy points often identify seven points.

Remember that we are assuming a perfect being and not a common human being. What is also interesting is that these points are not fixed at all, as is normally thought, but vary from individual to individual and from moment to moment.

Since all these seven forms of energy that characterize us "vibrate", we can think of ordering them according to a crescent scale.

The most subtle energy, the energy that vibrates beyond our possible comprehension, is definitely the *Inborn Voice*. It is an energy capable of acting as a bridge of communication between this world and something else.

Soon after it, we find the energy of emotions, which as we have seen is in direct proximity with our *Inborn Voice* and is, therefore, the only energy easily available to us that can somehow resonate with it.

Then come the energies that guarantee us movement, sexuality, and thought. Finally, the slowest energies are the vocality and the one that forms our body.

The vibration frequency is just an interesting fact and not directly related to the "speed" I'm talking about. It is useful to understand that these higher "speed" are also reflected in our world.

Everyone who has learned how to do some manual work, from writing to playing an instrument, from driving a car to dancing, has come to appreciate the different speeds at which the mind and body work.

In fact to learn how to write in block letters through the energy of the mind took years.

Now that this ability has been transmitted, by the phenomena of resonance, to the energy of movement, we can write at speeds unthinkable to a six-year-old child.

The same can be said of driving a car. At first, everything seemed to happen too quickly for the mind to be able to follow it, now probably everything happens automatically, without the mind taking care of it. This is because the energy of movement is much "faster" than that of thought.

Anyone who has learned any form of art, such as drawing, playing an instrument or singing, knows perfectly well how long it took to learn how to make the mechanical process linked to the chosen discipline "automatic".

However, this ability is not enough to define an "artist". In order to succeed in transforming a technical ability, even a flawless one, into an art form, it is necessary to make a further step and bring this ability to "resonate" even within emotions. Since we have seen that the emotions are a vibration very close to the *Inborn Voice*, it's really difficult to do so.

In my industry, that of voice and singing, it is increasingly rare to find someone who is able to move other people through the voice, although it is increasingly common to meet those who have awesome technical skills.

If the technique alone were enough to have a fantastic voice, today the computers would be perfectly able to simulate a human voice or the construction technique would be able to build violins capable of the magical sounds typical of those made by Stradivari.

Practically every vibration is surely able to "communicate", to transmit information, only to those vibrations that are at energy levels next to them, in closer "octaves".

You will easily understand the impossibility of communication there is, for example, between mind and emotions. They are two totally different worlds, incompatible.

In order for the mind to "understand" an emotion, it takes an intriguing tuning process between the different energies involved. We can give an example by talking about any of our senses. If we consider taste we can understand if we like something or not, but as soon as we try to consider this fact with the mind, we try to create comparisons and rankings.

The same can be done with sight, hearing and even touch. Emotion is able to give a "resonant" response, that is if the one we are interacting with resonates or not with something inside. It is not able to make comparisons. The mind, on the other hand, immediately tries to classify everything in very distinct categories. For example, sweet, salty, crunchy, disgusting, etc.

The mind simply cannot understand the nuances of an emotion because its vibration cannot contain all the necessary information. A bit like what we saw happening with the process of recording the sound of a violin, some of the original information is dispersed.

This "slowness" of the mind is also evident when something is planned with extreme precision, down to the smallest details, and then implemented. It can be a phone call, cooking a dish, going to the cinema or any other activity, even simple. The vibration produced by the program created by the mind, at a certain point will come into dissonance with the reality. For example the person called does not answer the phone, the smell of the cooked dish does not appeal or the queue to enter the parking lot of the cinema is tremendously long.

People generally feel the dissonance, but instead of listening to it they continue to blindly follow their own plan, generating emotions that are often unpleasant.

Going into the specifics of my work, many of the top managers who contact me, cannot address a speech, a meeting, an important presentation without first having made a detailed program that includes, as a game of chess, all the possible moves.

They are all more than prepared and have even followed specific training on how to speak in public, but it is enough that there is something unforeseen, of whatever nature, that their plan turns against them.

Despite all the effort put into the preparation, their expectations almost always seem not to be fulfilled. When they come to me, convinced that there is no practical solution to their problems, they are always amazed by the results they get when they learn to use the passion that comes from their *Inborn Voice* to deal with life and situations, without the mind pretending to control everything.

As I said, there exist twelve energies that characterize an evolved human being. I don't differentiate between higher and lower forms, since nothing about us can be "superior" to the *Inborn Voice* that characterizes us. Those who "think" that there may be something superior are simply using their heads, a very slow and imprecise organ, as we have seen so far.

I should like to conclude by saying a few words about the types of vibration that I omitted from above.

Some of them are very deep, others are more superficial. In order to develop them, all you need to do is go down *the way of the voice*, tuning in your entire being to your *Inborn Voice*. Everything else will be created naturally.

For this to happen, it is essential not only to "tune" all the internal vibrations, but also that they all participate equally in the creation of the same symphony. If someone devotes too much energy to developing a particular vibration, he or she will not have enough energy left to develop others.

When a person manages to develop all his vibrations in harmony with each other, somehow he turns into a kind of beautiful musical score capable of doing great things and everything he needs to continue to resonate in this world will be given easily and effortlessly.

At this point, we can only introduce the source of the above mentioned "energies", the one that allows us to exist. You will surely know that the energy needed to sustain the body comes from food. You may have also heard about many theories, diets, and ideologies related to food. I'm not interested in going into too much detail. The important thing is to understand that everything that exists in nature is some form of vibration, some form of musical symphony.

Vibrations don't exist only to communicate, to transmit a message, but also to provide energy or to allow excess energy to be disposed of.

Understood this concept, it becomes evident that the food we eat is only part of the vibrations we accumulate every day. We absorb energies through our ears listening to sounds, through our eyes looking at our surroundings, through our thoughts, focusing our minds on an idea, and so on. Even the air we breathe makes its contribution!

We have to be careful because not all vibrations, so to speak, "recharge": some are even able to debilitate us. Some will add to our disposal "thin" matter, others will subtract it. Some amplify a vibration, others neutralize it.

Anyone can argue that natural sounds, unspoiled landscapes, fresh food are "better" than technological alternatives, but you should not make the mistake of considering everything in the same way for everyone.

Each of us has a different *Inborn Voice* and will resonate in harmony with different vibrations. So it's a good idea to use the compass at our disposal, our *Inborn Voice*, to also understand what vibrations we absorb make us feel better and what vibrations make us feel worse.

In conclusion, man should first be educated to manage his essence and then instructed to participate actively in society because it is fundamental to understand that true knowledge is something vibrational and not something that can be learned through the intellect.

8
THE WAY OF THE VOICE

The way starts inside and reaches outside

If you have had the perseverance to get to this point by going through the whole book you are definitely already with one foot on *the way of the voice*. If you have taken a shortcut, nothing is lost, but it will take more time to understand whether or not you want to engage in this process.

The evolution of society has always been affected by the lack of proper use of the voice.

For historical, strategic or political reasons, human beings are not trained to use their voices to communicate with others. Typically, the voice is used incorrectly and almost always to try to convince the cognitive part of other people of something we want. Whether it's a sale, a sentimental proposal, a sports story, the voice is used almost exclusively to try to communicate to others our own fantastic vision of the world.

The result of this evolution is that the people of the modern era are progressively ceasing to communicate by voice. We all "talk" through messages, we chat, we write e-mails, we use social networks. The written form is preferred and abbreviations and symbolisms are used to make it even faster. That is not a bad thing in the absolute sense, but you will surely have noticed how many times this type of communication leads to misunderstandings, bad moods and unnecessary angry feelings.

You may have occasionally sent messages with several questions and received only the answer to the first one. At other times, you may have taken some facts for granted, assuming that the other party was aware of them, creating a misunderstanding. It may also have happened that the recipient did not respond immediately to a request, making the other party feel angry. These communication problems are all linked to the absurd claim that words are enough to communicate correctly to others.

You may have noticed that we use our voices less and less to communicate effectively with others. The intention of society is to create a kind of noisy isolation, immersing ourselves in rivers of words that often have no use and no substantial content.

We could also hypothesize that deep communication between two individuals is becoming extinct, giving way to functions that are completely useless to one's own personal evolution, such as giving voice to complaints or hanging ourselves from the facts of others.

Using the voice correctly is something more

than breathing life into the mouth to pronounce a more or less sensible sequence of words.

This book, although written by a vocal coach, does not pretend that people learn to use their voice by adopting some strange technique or prodigious form of breathing. Quite the opposite.

Having reached this point, it is my duty to make a clarification. You don't have to have an enviable voice or vocal technique to travel along *the way of the voice*, rather the whole process is more a tuning process with your own *Inborn Voice*. In fact, those who get a harmonious voice with prodigious resonances in their lives more quickly are usually those who have not had any previous experience of vocal training.

I have become famous as a Voice Guru because I can improve my clients' voices without ever using any vocalization exercises. One of the phrases that are often repeated in the testimonies I receive is summarized in something like "I don't understand how my voice has improved without ever having produced sounds".

Many of the people I work with, especially singers, come to me when they notice that something in their voice is no longer as it was before or, worse still, when some doctor has diagnosed the existence of some serious vocal problem.

Unfortunately, only those who use their voices at work worry about the symptoms that appear rhythmically in their vocals. The most common symptoms are frequent sore throats, sudden drops in voice, shortness of breath while speaking in front of an audience, sensations of dry mouth, stuttering or other flaws related to screaming words.

The symptoms that come from our phonatory system should never be underestimated.

If what you have read so far resonates with some symptom that reappears rhythmically, then the best advice I can give you is not to seek a solution in some traditional style vocal lesson. This type of lesson focuses mainly on tuning the voice to unnatural musical notes through the use of more or less imaginative and harmful vocalizations. Of course, I don't even consider those who claim to teach how to sing with a

Karaoke style session, because that is the sure way to ruin your vocal cords, even when you only do it as a hobby or for fun.

A constant that accompanies my adventure in the world of vocal coaching from the beginning is that many people are convinced that with some secret exercise their voice or their life problems, will magically disappear.

There are no exercises, and there can't exist an exercise able to transform your voice into something your mind consider wonderful or that can teach you how to use it better than Mother Nature has already done.

There are only exercises that help you to remove, to eliminate, the incorrect way of using the voice you have learned until now.

You may have noticed there is no newborn baby that "loses" its voice for having cried too much, there is no newborn baby that screams under volume, there is not even a newborn baby that will stop crying at command.

I'm not a magical creature and I can't even do magic on command: I can only help people to return to use the perfect tool they had at their disposal when they were created, removing all the bad things learned over the years and returning in perfect harmony with their *Inborn Voice*.

Another point I would like to make is that the *Inborn Voice* communication does not use words. This is nothing that has been described so far by others. It has nothing to do with what in psychology is defined as "internal dialogue" between different personalities.

In the book, I specifically chose to speak always and only about *Inborn Voice* to avoid the inevitable abuses that will come after its publication. Be wary of anyone who starts talking about an innate voice and not about *Inborn Voice*. At best, something different is being referred to.

The goal of my work as a vocal coach is always just one: to identify and make flourish the talent already present in my client. Talent is something you can't put inside a person, but you can only pull it out, which is why I have so many successes in my work.

Every musical instrument must first be built,

then tuned and only then can it be played.

I work with people and it is easy to understand they have already been "built" by Mother Nature. Clearly, when they come to me they already have years of more or less "incorrect use" behind them. I can't boast that I've done anything about their construction, even though I treat them all with the love and firmness of a mother.

My work begins with selecting the people I'd like to work with, those in whom I'd hear the *Inborn Voice* ringing loudly. Although this may seem cruel, it is the only way to work seriously and without fooling people.

Don't worry! One step at a time I am preparing others to master my method, each chosen according to the fundamental note of their own *Inborn Voice*, so as to have an orchestra available to further spread this message to the world.

Once I have started working with my client I try to "repair" the instrument in front of me to bring it back to its original condition.

For the repair to be perfect, I need full

commitment, dedication, and confidence from the client. Without these elements, there is no possibility of hearing the *Inborn Voice* resonate.

Typically, my clients are only interested in improving their vocal skills, so many of them feel satisfied with the results they get without wanting to investigate these aspects further. Once their immediate problem has been "solved", they typically finish the training without willing to go deeper, even if the work done up to that moment will continue to shine for a long time.

The next step in my work is "tuning". This passage is typically what faces those who want to sing. I try to find the best resonance to make the voice come out as painlessly as possible along with the emotions and, eventually, also along with their *Inborn Voice*. To tune a human being is a complex operation that requires all his collaboration and much love. The intervention takes place in a few moments, completely unconsciously, but it takes a long time to settle and strengthen.

If a musician mismatches his or her guitar, it will produce annoying, cacophonic sounds, but it's an easily correctable situation. However, if the tuning is really off, it can lead to the breaking or destruction of a string or even the instrument. The musical instrument cannot rebel against the bad "tuner".

The same happens with people. If the "tuner" doesn't know what he is doing, he risks leading them to produce sounds that disturb or dissonate with their *Inborn Voice* or even contribute to its destruction.

Having made these points, it is necessary to separate the superficial aspect of the voice, the one that I deal with daily in my work, from something different that is the subject of this book.

Walking along t*he way of the voice* is a bit like leaving for a trip. What are the things you do before leaving? Prepare suitcases, medicines, documents, tickets, delegate to those who will take care of the house, plants and any animals. These probably are some of the things that you will all have thought about.

Actually, when you get to this point of the trip you already have your ticket in hand and you know exactly where you are going.

I am referring to the previous moments. You will think first about how much you can spend, then you will choose a destination. These are all classic operations of those who plan a journey with the energy of the mind. But *the way of the voice* starts from the *Inborn Voice*, several "octaves" away from the mind. The only thing you can do to go down *the way of the voice* is to choose to leave. Everything else will come by itself, as if by magic.

In my life, I have traveled practically all over the planet in search of new sounds and different vibrations to expand my knowledge and to make my work even more unique.

I have visited incredible places, met wonderful people and cultures. I have beautiful memories of the Maoris, of their unique way of using their voice and body: participating in an Aka in person is a truly vibrant experience.

Those who know me know that I never make organized vacation trips. I pick up the vibration that calls me to somewhere, buy tickets, find out what I'll find and then go. Nothing fixed or programmed. Do it by yourself tourist, no travel packages or agencies involved.

I follow vibrations. The same vibrations that led me to live and work in Boston, to meet many people who are now helping me to bring this message to resound throughout the world.

We have arrived at the key point.

The way of the Voice.

I chose to use the term "way" because it expresses well the concept of movement, evolution, and solitude. "Street" would suggest an idea of something crowded, where you can meet others, while "path" made me think of something dark and narrow.

I chose to use the term "voice" because it is a way made of resonant vibrations with the *Inborn Voice*, not because it is somehow connected to the use of the actual voice.

The way of the voice exists for sure, but it is not something that can be shown on the pages of a book. As we have seen in previous chapters, its existence shines through several of the oldest texts available to us. It has never been kept secret and is in no way to be considered as something to be kept hidden.

The way of the voice, even if it must be traveled entirely alone with one's own strength, can't be found without the help of someone who has already traveled at least some part of it.

It can only be taken with the help of someone who consciously chooses to "give up" and share part of the pure "matter" that he has managed to collect for himself. Only in this manner is possible to trigger in the other the vibration useful to get back in touch with the compass that we were given: our *Inborn Voice*.

As I explained in the book, in order for a vibration to occur it is always necessary to have at one's disposal some kind of matter that can resonate with it.

Once you start the process, as long as you stay "tuned in" to your *Inborn Voice*, the way opens before you, one step at a time.

It is a very long journey through a beautiful place, perhaps now gloomy and scary. Being at the entrance of *the way of the voice* for the first time is a bit like being in Tokyo and wanting to go somewhere, for example to the famous park of Odaiba. One would find oneself asking a local for directions, without knowing anything about the Japanese language, perhaps right in front of a sign, as big as a bus, which indicates which is the direction to go. There is no way to understand Japanese or to decode the signs if you do not know the Japanese language. You need to learn a bit of Japanese, or find someone who knows already the language of the rising sun and acts as an interpreter until you learn.

Sure, learning Japanese takes a long time, it's not something you can do in a day, a week or a month. Learning does not require only time; you need a lot of determination and personal passion.

Don't worry. For my part, you will receive all the teachings you need to recognize and stay away from debilitating vibrations, as well as identify and follow those that resonate.

The way of the voice is not a straight route, but neither is it an obstacle course.

The further you go, the clearer you get the idea of what to expect at the end of the journey: your own personal fulfillment, as it was conceived from the moment of your birth.

The way of the voice is something extremely private, in fact it starts in the deepest part of each of us, right at our *Inborn Voice*, and ends in the outside world.

To reach it you have to follow inscrutable paths that no logic can ever understand. It is a journey for which you only know the starting point and you cannot choose your destination. As with quantum particles, if only you try to impose your will, the way changes immediately or disappears from before your eyes.

The way of the voice knows no shortcuts and no guide can accompany you along the route. The only thing you need is education to learn how to listen to your *Inborn Voice* so you have a compass able to tell you when there's resonance and when it's missing. Obviously, you will also need to have faith in your compass.

Do you want to know what the original meaning of the word "faith" is? The word *faith* finds its origins in the name of a string of a musical instrument and its most philosophical meaning is to "fulfill to a promise," a somewhat romantic way to "not lie to ourselves". As you can see, once again an ancient concept linked to a vibration.

By learning how to use your compass and having faith in its resonance capabilities, anyone can become a miraculous adventurer.

The best place to hide a secret is on everyone's lips. An ancient legend tells that once human beings were Gods. Our creator, seeing the misuse that humans made of the power he gifted, decided to deprive us of it and then he hides it. The creator tried to hide it on the tops of the highest mountains, but humans climbed them all to find it. Then he hid it in the depths of the earth, but humans dug very deep wells to recover it. He finally tried to hide it even in the depths of the oceans, but nothing. The humans found it there too. There was no place on earth where humans would not seek. So the creator decided to hide this power in a place where no man would ever have looked: in his own heart.

Our *Inborn Voice* is still there, reachable.

Now practically no human being dreams of continuing to seek that magical power.

Serendipity allows some to get in touch with this power for a few moments, but not knowing how to use it, nothing wonderful happens.

Those who have so far grasped most of this secret have unfortunately filtered it through the vibration of the mind, in a very twisted and limited way, tying it to vibrations such as "wealth" or "happiness".

In reality, anyone who walks *the way of the voice* will resonate with the melody of their evolution, but they will do so in mysterious and unpredictable ways.

It will certainly bring to fruition the talent, multiply it and make it blossom. But this does not mean, in the strongest term, becoming rich, being famous or living a prosperous life.

Once people start tuning to their *Inborn Voice*, everyone will receive everything needs to grow loud and clear, nothing less, nothing more.

The profound meaning of t*he way of the voice* is very simple: everything that man seeks in the world has already been given to him and is hidden within himself. It is useless to seek love, acceptance, security, happiness, money, fortune and whatever else. What you can find is already there and everything else will come as a consequence.

If we are able to find in ourselves our birth vibration, our *Inborn Voice*, everything we were desperately searching for in this world so far it will no longer seem interesting to us. Hiding the little guru in the depths of each of us was a smart move so that whoever is able to find it along *the way of the voice* will automatically obtain the wisdom necessary not to abuse the gift found.

Each existing philosophy today revolves around a unique road, different from that of the others. None of these roads is right or wrong, but they are all too crowded and they pretend to lead from the outside world to the inside one.

The philosophy of *the way of the voice* is exactly the opposite. It is strictly intimate and personal, born from within and leads outward, so that everyone will bring his personal gift into the world we share.

Music, poetry, painting and any other form of art are always the expressions of something that was born inside someone and that has become evident in the physical world. These are all works capable of moving something inside, of triggering a vibration.

If we were to use our minds to judge a work of art, we would find it childish, imprecise, unsuitable or even stupid. This is an obvious difference between the philosophies that try to shape the thought and the philosophy of the *Inborn Voice* that respects the vibrations and uses the mind as an instrument and not as a commander.

The mind often has the strange ability to act in complicity with the neutralizing energies and always tries to turn off any vibration that departs from the status quo. Even in science, a field related to the mind, we find striking examples of innovators who have had the courage to bring into the world part of their *Inborn Voice*, while going against the rationality of the majority, who most likely did not consider them anything but fools.

Ultimately t*he way of voice* leads to awareness, for what it really is. In fact, the origin of the word *awareness* refers to something extremely intimate, yet of vital importance. It is not a word that can be related in any way to the mind, it has nothing to do with knowledge or intellect. The mind, the intellect is something too slow and clumsy to be able to have the intuition of what awareness really is.

Awareness is a condition of perfect and deep harmony with everything, that's why I always talk about *Vocal Realignment*™ with those looking for their own *Inborn Voice*.

The beauty of awareness, the true one, is that it rises spontaneously from within and in no way can it be "slipped in" from outside.

The awareness coming from your *Inborn Voice* will help you orient yourself towards the choices of the future, so that you can proceed quickly, not in the direction that the mind considers "right", but in the one that resonates most with what has been given to you.

The way of the voice at first leads the human being to no longer lie to himself, it proceeds towards personal awareness and then reaches universal awareness.

I hope that this book will turn into a seed capable of finding in you fertile ground on which to grow strong and luxuriant. Only in this way, the resonance of this humble message of mine will be able to spread and bring happiness throughout the planet.

Acknowledgments

Although each of us wants to do everything by himself, without ever asking for help, perhaps it is my destiny to achieve great results and successes by sharing it with other special people.

I begin with my grandparents, who taught me sweetness, elegance, transparency, and humility. Then this love for me and for everyone else was consolidated thanks to my parents, who continue to give me every day the love and strength to keep going along my personal way of the voice. Having a daughter on the other side of the ocean is not easy when you love so much. To them, I owe my determination, my strength and my unquestionable pride in being what I am, "no matter what they say".

Another big thank you goes to my husband who listens to all my wishes and guides me with care and respect in the world of technology.

I thank all the people who directly or indirectly have pushed me first and then accompanied me in the drafting of this book. Naming them all would be impossible, but I am sure that their essence will shine through between the lines.

I would also like to thank you, dear reader, who have patiently come to read this page: remember that it is not important to find an answer, but to find the right question!

Contacts

If you have questions about the topics covered in this book or if you want to point out some inaccuracies, the author can be reached through her websites:

https://www.inbornvoice.com

https://www.findyourvoice.guru

or through the various social media:

Twitter **@mylenaofficial**

Instagram **@mylenaofficial**

LinkedIn: **MylenaVocalCoach**

Facebook: **MylenaVocalCoach**

Mylena organizes conferences, workshops, and retreats around the world. You'll find all the information on her websites and social media. Contact her if you're interested in having her for a workshop or a lecture in your city.

Commitment permitting, Mylena always answers personally to all polite e-mail requests.

www.ingramcontent.com/pod-product-compliance
Lightning Source LLC
Chambersburg PA
CBHW020421010526
44118CB00010B/357